GROWING FROM DEPRESSION

Happiness is good for the body, but it is grief which develops the strengths of the mind.

—Marcel Proust, *In Search of Lost Time*

GROWING FROM DEPRESSION

Dr Neel Burton

Acheron Press

Flectere si nequeo superos
Acheronta movebo

© Acheron Press 2017

Published by Acheron Press

A CIP catalogue record for this book is available from the British Library.

ISBN 978 0 9929127 6 5

Typeset by Phoenix Photosetting, Chatham, Kent, United Kingdom
Printed and bound by SRP Limited, Exeter, Devon, United Kingdom

About the author

Dr Neel Burton is a psychiatrist, philosopher, writer, and wine lover who lives and teaches in Oxford, England.

He is a Fellow of Green-Templeton College, Oxford, and the recipient of the Society of Authors' Richard Asher Prize, the British Medical Association's Young Authors' Award, the Medical Journalists' Association Open Book Award, and a Best in the World Gourmand Award.

His other books include:

The Meaning of Madness
Heaven and Hell: The Psychology of the Emotions
Hide and Seek: The Psychology of Self-Deception
The Art of Failure: The Anti Self-Help Guide

www.neelburton.com

About Acheron Press

Acheron Press was established in 2008 by Neel Burton to publish challenging books without the constraints of a commercial, sales-driven approach.

The name 'Acheron' was inspired by a verse from the *Aeneid*:

Flectere si nequeo superos, Acheronta movebo

The line is often translated as, 'If I cannot bend Heaven, I shall move Hell', and was chosen by Freud as the epigraph to his *Interpretation of Dreams*.

According to the psychoanalyst Bruno Bettelheim, the line encapsulates Freud's theory that people who have no control over the outside world turn inward to the underworld of their own minds.

Contents

Introduction

Growing From Depression—rather than, say, *Recovering from Depression* or *Defeating Depression*—is a counterintuitive, perhaps even provocative, title for a book on depression. I chose it for what I think are three very good reasons.

First, I wanted to challenge the general perception of people with depression. Rather than being 'lazy' or 'losers', they are often, as I will argue, among some of the most ambitious, truthful, and courageous of all people.

Second, while I would never wish it on anyone, depression can challenge us to identify and address long-standing life problems, opening us out onto a much brighter future.

Third, and perhaps most obviously, the journey out of depression is one of learning: learning about oneself, of course, but also learning life skills such as managing stress and coping with boredom, and, above all, learning to rediscover the little things that make life worth living and loving.

In emphasizing the good that can come from depression, I hope to encourage and empower you to tackle the feelings of hopelessness and helplessness that are the core of the condition, and, like Baron Munchausen, to pull yourself out of the swamp by your own bootstraps.

As poor concentration is a common feature of depression, I have divided the self-help section into short, self-contained modules, enabling you, should you so wish, to dip in and out of the book, and to focus on whatever seems most interesting or useful. I have also tried to be as succinct as possible.

I wish you the best of luck on your quest.

All that is gold does not glitter,
Not all those who wander are lost;
The old that is strong does not wither,
Deep roots are not reached by the frost.

From the ashes a fire shall be woken,
A light from the shadows shall spring;
Renewed shall be blade that was broken,
The crownless again shall be king.

—JRR Tolkien, *The Fellowship of the Ring*

Part 1

Understanding depression

1

What is depression?

Many people use the term 'depression' to refer to normal disappointment or sadness, and there can be little doubt that the concept of depression as a mental disorder, that is, a biological illness of the brain, has been unhelpfully overextended to include all manner of human suffering. The concept of depression as a mental disorder may be helpful for the more severe and intractable cases treated by psychiatrists (medical doctors like myself who specialize in the diagnosis and treatment of mental disorders), but probably not for the majority of cases, which, for the most part, are mild and short-lived and readily interpreted in terms of life circumstances, human nature, or the human condition.

Figures for the lifetime incidence of depression (the chance of any one person developing depression in the course of her lifetime) vary according to the criteria used to define 'depression', that is, according to where we draw the line between illness and 'normality'. Using the criteria in the influential American classification of mental disorders, the DSM-5, the lifetime incidence of depression is about 15 per cent, and the point prevalence (the chance of any one person suffering from depression at this point in time) is about 5 per cent—which still seems very high for a biological illness of the brain. Depression, as defined by DSM-5, is so common that the costs of treating it exceed the combined costs of treating hypertension and diabetes.

Why is it so difficult to define 'depression'? If someone is suspected of having malaria, a blood sample can be taken and examined under a microscope for malarial parasites of the genus

Plasmodium; and if someone appears to have suffered a stroke, a brain scan can be taken to look for evidence of obstruction of an artery in the brain. In contrast, depression, in common with other mental disorders, cannot be defined and diagnosed according to its physical cause (aetiology) or effect (pathology), but only according to its manifestations or symptoms. This means that a doctor cannot base a diagnosis of depression on any objective criterion such as a blood test or brain scan, but only on her subjective interpretation of the nature and severity of the patient's symptoms. If some of these symptoms appear to tally with the diagnostic criteria for depression, which are rather loose, then the doctor is able to justify a diagnosis of depression.

The problem here is that the definition of 'depression' is circular: the concept of depression is defined according to the symptoms of depression, which in turn are defined according to the concept of depression. For this reason, it is impossible to be certain that the concept of depression maps onto any distinct disease entity, particularly since a diagnosis of depression can apply to anything from mild depression to depressive psychosis and stupor, and overlap with several other concepts and constructs including dysthymia, adjustment disorder, and anxiety disorders. One of the consequences of our 'menu of symptoms' approach to diagnosing depression is that two people with absolutely no symptoms in common can both end up with the same diagnosis of depression. For this reason especially, the concept of depression as a mental disorder has been charged with being little more than a socially constructed dustbin for all manner of human suffering.

People frequently speak of normal disappointment or sadness as 'depression', as in, 'Jack is pretty depressed (upset) about failing his exam.' They even apply the term to undesirable outcomes or states of affairs, as in, 'Thinking about global warming is pretty depressing (dispiriting, disheartening).' Naturally, when things get out of hand, they come to believe that they (and others) are suffering from what is, in the end, a mental disorder. By pushing them towards doctors and drugs, their belief can prevent them from identifying and addressing the important life problems that underlie their distress, and so from developing a deeper and more refined appreciation of themselves and the world around them. This book is for everyone with low mood, whether or not they are suffering from clinical depression, which, for many people, may be a moot point.

What does depression feel like?

The symptoms of clinical depression, as defined by DSM-5, fall into three groups: core symptoms, psychological symptoms, and physical symptoms (Table 1.1).

Table 1.1:   Symptoms of depression

Core symptoms	Low mood
	Loss of interest or pleasure
Psychological symptoms	Poor concentration
	Poor self-esteem
	Inappropriate guilt
	Recurring thoughts of death or suicide
Physical symptoms	Sleep disturbance
	Loss of appetite and weight loss
	Fatigability
	Agitation or retardation

The **core symptoms** of depression are low mood and loss of interest or pleasure. Although these symptoms are present in the vast majority of cases, some people with depression never complain of low mood but instead present with symptoms such as tiredness or poor concentration, or simply an inability to function, that is, to do the things that they used to do.

The **psychological symptoms** of depression include poor concentration, poor self-esteem, inappropriate guilt, and recurring thoughts of death or suicide. Poor concentration is the norm, and the person may find it very difficult to focus on everyday activities such as making conversation, reading the news, or watching television. As a result, she may find it difficult to remember or recall things, and come to the conclusion that she is losing her memory. However, while depression does affect concentration, it does not directly affect memory.

The **physical symptoms** of depression typically affect the areas of sleep, appetite, and the libido. The person may find it difficult to fall asleep, or wake up in the morning feeling un-refreshed. In some cases, she may wake up unusually early, a phenomenon referred to as 'early morning waking'. She may eat considerably less than usual, not only because she no longer feels like eating (loss of appetite), but also because she no longer enjoys her food, and/or because she no longer has the energy or motivation to prepare or eat it. She may have no desire for romance or sexual intercourse, or even simple conversation, which, in the long run, may undermine her relationship and the support that it provides. If you are in a relationship with someone with depression, remember that your partner still has feelings for you, even if her illness prevents her from expressing them. Looking ahead, your patience and understanding in a time of need is very likely to deepen your relationship.

Many people with depression also suffer from **anxiety**, either as part of the depression or in the form of a separate and diagnosable anxiety disorder. For more on anxiety in depression, see page 25.

In contrast to normal sadness or stress, the symptoms of depression vary little from day to day and barely respond to changing circumstances. For example, a depressed person who normally loves Italian food will not brighten up even upon being taken to her favourite pizzeria.

According to DSM-5, for a diagnosis of depression to be made, five or more symptoms from a list similar to the one in Table 1.1 must have been present for a period of two weeks or more.

At least one of the symptoms must be either depressed mood or loss of interest or pleasure, and the symptoms must be associated with significant distress or impairment. The diagnostician must also exclude physical states that can masquerade as depression such as thinning of the blood (anaemia) or an underactive thyroid gland.

How bad can it get?

Mild depression, if it can be counted as depression, is the most common form of depression. People with mild depression complain of feeling low, tired, and/or stressed or anxious, but some frame their experience more in terms of how it is affecting their everyday life. For example, they may say that they can no longer concentrate on their job, or that they no longer enjoy the company of their partner or children. People with mild depression might harbour suicidal thoughts, but these are usually fleeting and fragmentary, and acts of self-harm are uncommon.

Moderate depression is the classic 'textbook description' of depression. Many if not most of the symptoms of depression, including the physical symptoms, are present to such an intense degree that the person finds it difficult if not impossible to fulfil her professional, marital, parental, and other social obligations. Suicidal thoughts are common, and may in some cases be acted upon.

Severe depression is relatively uncommon. It is characterized by intense negative feelings and physical agitation or retardation (slowing down of speech and movements). Retardation is more typical than agitation, although in some cases a person may suffer alternately with both agitation and retardation. On occasion, retardation may be so severe that the person is mute and stuporous, that is, motionless and unreactive. The risk of suicide is significant, and may actually increase as the person gets better and develops the motivation and energy to act on her suicidal thoughts.

Whereas most people with moderate depression are treated in general practice, people with severe depression are much more likely to be referred to specialist psychiatric services.

William Styron, the author of *Sophie's Choice*, wrote about his experience of severe depression in *Darkness Visible*:

> *In depression, this faith in deliverance, in ultimate restoration, is absent. The pain is unrelenting, and what makes the condition intolerable is the foreknowledge that no remedy will come—not in a day, an hour, a month, or a minute. If there is mild relief, one knows that it is only temporary; more pain will follow. It is hopelessness even more than pain that crushes the soul. So the decision-making of everyday life involves not, as in normal affairs, shifting from one annoying situation to another less annoying—or from discomfort to relative comfort, or from boredom to activity—but moving from pain to pain. One does not abandon, even briefly, one's bed of nails, but is attached to it wherever one goes.*

However severe your condition, and whether or not it meets, or has once met, the diagnostic criteria for clinical depression, you will find at least some of the advice in this book helpful. Instead of getting bogged down with diagnoses, let's focus our minds on the road ahead.

What is psychosis?

A significant minority of people with usually severe depression also suffer from psychotic symptoms, that is, delusions and/or hallucinations. Severe depression with psychotic symptoms is sometimes referred to as 'psychotic depression' or 'depressive psychosis'.

A **delusion** is defined as 'a strongly held belief that is not amenable to logic or persuasion and that is out of keeping with its holder's background or culture'. Although delusions need not be false, the process by which they are arrived at is usually bizarre and illogical.

Psychotic symptoms in depression are usually in keeping with a depressive outlook. Delusions are commonly along themes of guilt or poverty. Delusions of guilt involve the belief that one has committed a crime or sinned greatly, for instance, by being personally responsible for an earthquake or terrorist attack that has been in the news. Delusions of poverty involve the belief that one is being, or has been, ruined, for instance, by being defrauded by a relative or pursued by a horde of creditors. Delusions can also take on 'nihilistic' overtones. *Nihil* is Latin for 'nothing', and nihilistic delusions involve the belief that one is about to be reduced to nothing, that is, to die or suffer a personal catastrophe, or even that one is already dead. Cotard's syndrome is the combination of nihilistic delusions with somatic delusions, that is, delusions about the body. For instance, a person might believe that her guts are putrefying, or that she has lost all her blood or internal organs. Paranoid delusions, religious delusions, and delusions on other themes are also possible.

A **hallucination** is defined as 'a sense perception that arises in the absence of an external stimulus'. Hallucinations involve hearing, seeing, smelling, tasting, or feeling things that are not actually there. The most common hallucinations are auditory, involving voices and sounds. The person may hear one or several voices, either talking to her (second-person—'you'— voices) or about her (third-person—'she'—voices). The voices are often mocking or attacking, seeking to undermine the person's self-esteem or entrench feelings of guilt or hopelessness. Voices that order the person to do certain things are called 'command hallucinations', and may goad her into harming herself, or, more unusually, harming other people. Voices can be highly distressing, especially if they involve threats or abuse, or if they are loud and incessant. However, not all voices are distressing, and some, such as the voices of old acquaintances, dead ancestors, or guardian angels, can be a source of comfort or reassurance.

Aside from severe depression, psychotic symptoms can also occur in a number of other states and conditions, most notably schizophrenia, mania (bipolar disorder), delirium, and drug intoxication.

Psychosis corresponds closely to the general public's idea of 'madness'. Feelings of fear and anxiety towards people with psychosis are reinforced by selective reporting in the media of the rare headline tragedies involving people with (usually untreated) mental illness, most often schizophrenia. The reality is that most people with psychosis are no more dangerous than you or me. All the opposite, in fact: they are exposed and vulnerable, and far more likely to threaten themselves, whether through self-harm, neglect, or openness to exploitation.

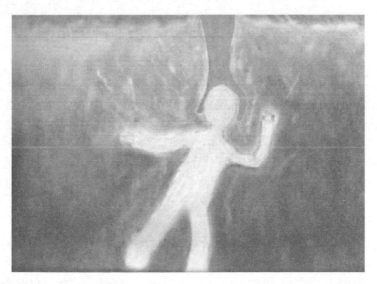

Figure 1.1: Crayon drawing by an in-patient suffering from severe depression with psychotic symptoms. She is drowning, and each time she struggles near the surface, it feels as though she is being pushed back down again. She went on to make a full recovery.

2

Who suffers from depression?

Depression has become increasingly common in industrialized countries. In the UK and US, the lifetime incidence of depression (the chance of any one person developing depression in the course of her lifetime) is usually quoted at around 15 per cent, and the point prevalence (the chance of any one person suffering from depression at this point in time) at around 5 per cent, but, as discussed in Chapter 1, these figures can vary quite considerably depending on where we decide to draw the line between 'illness' and 'normality'.

Male versus female

Such headline figures mask an uneven gender distribution, with women twice as likely to be diagnosed with depression than men. The reasons for this asymmetry are unclear, and thought to be in part biological, in part psychological, and in part sociocultural.

Possible biological explanations: Compared to men, women are subjected to fluctuating hormone levels, particularly around the times of childbirth and the menopause. Beyond this, they might also have a stronger genetic predisposition to developing depression.

Possible psychological explanations: Women are more ruminative than men, that is, they tend to think through things more. In contrast, men are more likely to respond to life problems with stoicism, anger, or alcohol and drug misuse. Women also tend to be more invested in relationships, and so more affected by relationship issues.

Possible sociocultural explanations: Women come under greater stress than men. In addition to going to work just like men, they are often expected to bear most of the burden of maintaining the family home, looking after the children, and caring for older relatives—and, after all that, still have to put up with all the sexism! Women live longer than men, and extreme old age is associated with bereavement, loneliness, ill health, and precarity. Finally, women are more likely to seek out a diagnosis of depression than men. They are more likely to consult a doctor and more likely to discuss their feelings with the doctor. Conversely, doctors, both male and female, may be more inclined to diagnose depression in a woman.

Young versus old

Depression can present at any age, but is most common in middle age in women (particularly around the time of the menopause), and in old age in men. It is relatively uncommon in children, or presents differently, for example, as behavioural disturbance. The point prevalence of depression by age and sex is graphically illustrated in Figure 2.1.

Depression around the world

There are important geographical variations in the prevalence of depression, and these can in large part be accounted for by sociocultural rather than biological factors.

In traditional societies, emotional distress is more likely to be interpreted as an indicator of the need to address important life problems rather than as a mental disorder requiring professional treatment. Many linguistic communities, for example, in India, Korea, and Nigeria, do not even have a word for 'depression', and many people from traditional societies with what may be construed as depression instead present with physical complaints

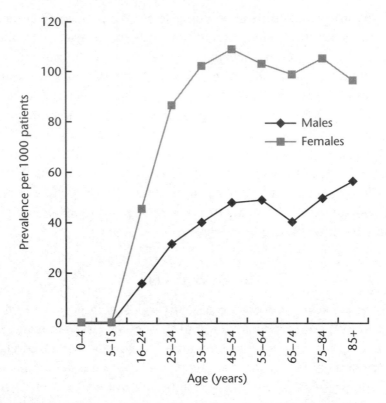

Figure 2.1:   Point prevalence of 'treated depression' by age and sex.

such as fatigue, headache, or chest pain. Punjabi women who have recently immigrated to the UK and given birth find it baffling that a health visitor should pop round to check their mood: it had never crossed their minds that giving birth could be anything but a joyous event.

Being much more exposed to the concept of depression, people in modern societies such as the UK and US are far more likely to interpret their distress in terms of depression and to seek out a diagnosis of the illness. At the same time, groups with vested interests actively promote the notion of saccharine happiness as a natural, default state, and of human distress as a mental disorder.

In her book, *Depression in Japan*, anthropologist Junko Kitanaka reports that, until relatively recently, depression (*utsubyō*) had remained largely unknown to the Japanese. Between 1999 and 2008, the diagnosis of depression more than doubled as psychiatrists and pharmaceutical companies urged people to re-interpret their distress in terms of the illness. Depression, says Kitanaka, is now one of the most frequently cited reasons for taking sick leave, and has been 'transformed from a rare disease to one of the most talked about illnesses in recent Japanese history'.

Another reason for the important geographical variations in the prevalence of depression may lie in the nature of modern societies, which have become increasingly individualistic and divorced from traditional values. For many people living in our society, life can seem both suffocating and far removed, lonely even and especially among the multitudes, and not only meaningless but absurd. By encoding their distress in terms of a mental disorder, our society may be subtly implying that the problem lies not with itself but with them as fragile and failing individuals. Of course, many people prefer to buy into this reductive explanation than to confront their existential angst. But thinking of their unhappiness in terms of an illness or chemical imbalance can prevent people from acknowledging the important life problems that are at the root of their distress, and so prevent them from growing, and from healing.

Depression and creativity

If you are suffering with depression, you are in very good company. Many of the most creative and insightful people who ever lived suffered from depression or a state that could have met the DSM-5 criteria for major depressive disorder. They include the politicians Winston Churchill and Abraham Lincoln; the poets Charles Baudelaire, Elizabeth Bishop, Hart Crane, Emily Dickinson, Sylvia Plath, and Rainer Maria Rilke; the thinkers Michel Foucault, William James, John Stuart Mill, Isaac Newton, Friedrich Nietzsche, and Arthur Schopenhauer; and the writers Agatha Christie, Charles Dickens, William Faulkner, Graham Greene, Leo Tolstoy, Evelyn Waugh, and Tennessee Williams— and the list goes on and on.

To quote the writer Marcel Proust, who himself suffered from depression, 'Happiness is good for the body, but it is grief which develops the strengths of the mind.'

> *When the shadow of the sash appeared on the curtains it was between seven and eight o'clock and then I was in time again, hearing the watch. It was Grandfather's and when Father gave it to me he said I give you the mausoleum of all hope and desire; it's rather excruciatingly apt that you will use it to gain the reducto absurdum of all human experience which can fit your individual needs no better than it fitted his or his father's. I give it to you not that you may remember time, but that you might forget it now and then for a moment and not spend all your breath trying to conquer it. Because no battle is ever won he said. They are not even fought. The field only reveals to man his own folly and despair, and victory is an illusion of philosophers and fools.*

—William Faulkner, *The Sound and the Fury* (1929)

3

What causes depression?

The role of genes

First-degree relatives (parents, siblings, and children) of a person with depression are three times more likely to suffer from depression than the average person. However, the makeup of our minds has much in common with that of our first-degree relatives, as does our social environment, meaning that this three-fold increase cannot simply be imputed to genes.

A better understanding of the role of genes in depression comes from twin studies, and more particularly from comparing the prevalence of depression in identical twins (who have 100 per cent of their genes in common) to that in non-identical twins (who have only 50 per cent of their genes in common). If one of a pair of identical twins develops depression, the chance of the other one also developing depression is 46 per cent or almost 1 in 2. But if one of a pair of non-identical twins develops depression, the chance of the other one also developing depression is only about 20 per cent, or 1 in 5. So genes do play a significant role in depression, but they are only part of the story: if they were the whole story, the chance of the second identical twin also developing depression would be a neat 100%.

The stress-vulnerability model

What's more, there is no one gene that can be said to predispose to depression. Rather, there are several genes that are independent of one another, and that, taken together, make a person more or less vulnerable to developing the condition.

A person who is highly vulnerable to developing depression but has a peaceful and comfortable life may never actually succumb to the condition, whereas a person who is much less vulnerable but who often comes under severe or prolonged stress may suffer repeated episodes.

It is just the same with other conditions such as heart disease or diabetes. Every person inherits a certain complement of genes that makes her more or less vulnerable to developing heart disease. But a person who eats healthily, exercises regularly, and never smokes is likely to remain healthy almost regardless of her vulnerability. Even if she does develop heart disease, she will do so at an older age and enjoy a better outcome.

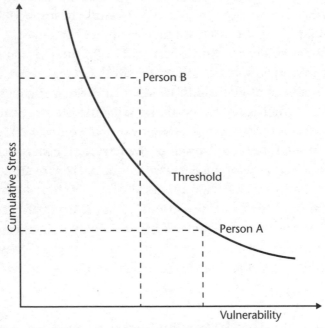

Figure 3.1: The stress-vulnerability model of depression. A person develops depression when the stress that she faces becomes greater than her genetically determined ability to cope with it. Person A is highly vulnerable to developing depression but suffers only moderate stress and so does not reach the threshold for the condition. In contrast, Person B, though only moderately vulnerable, is subjected to very high stress and so crosses the threshold.

Understanding stress

Stress is often related to life events, that is, important events such as losing a loved one, going through a divorce, or falling ill. Life events need not be negative: getting married, having a baby, moving house, or going on holiday can count as significant life events for some people, in so far as they can be highly stressful. Life events are subjective: what counts as a life event for me does not necessarily count as a life event for you, and vice versa.

I'd like to make three more points about stress. First, the relationship between life events and depression is a very complex one, as life events can both cause and be caused by depression. For example, if a person cannot concentrate, she is much more likely to lose her job or crash her car.

Second, although life events are a major source of stress, most of the stress that a person experiences on a daily basis comes from seemingly smaller 'background' stressors such as constant deadlines, long and difficult commutes, tense relationships, painful memories, poor housing, unpaid bills, isolation, and discrimination. The cumulative effect of all these background stressors can easily exceed that of any single life event, and may alone suffice to tip a person into depression.

My final point about stress is that different people are able to handle different amounts of it. The amount of stress that a person can handle is related not only to her genetic makeup, but also to her thinking and coping styles and to her social skills. People with positive coping and thinking styles and good social skills have the resources to diffuse stressful situations, for example, by doing something about them, putting them into context and perspective, or simply talking about them and 'sharing the burden'.

Alcohol and drugs

As with stress, substance misuse (misuse of alcohol or drugs) can both cause and result from depression. Many people with depression turn to substances to relieve their symptoms. These substances may blunt or mask the symptoms in the short term, but in the longer term they are likely to make the symptoms worse and lead to more frequent and severe relapses. A vicious circle takes hold wherein the more a person uses substances to mask her symptoms, the worse her symptoms become; and the worse her symptoms become, the more she uses substances to mask her symptoms. Meanwhile, she is unable to find the help that she needs or engage with the life problems that underlie her depression. If anything, she is adding to her life problems by undermining her health, career, finances, and relationships.

4

How is depression diagnosed?

As discussed in Chapter 1, depression is difficult to define and diagnose, and the diagnostic criteria are fairly loose.

A doctor normally reaches a diagnosis of depression by obtaining a detailed picture of the person's background and problems.

One of the doctor's main concerns is to rule out conditions that can lead to depression such as an anxiety disorder, alcohol misuse, or an underactive thyroid gland, because such 'secondary' depression is best treated by treating the primary, or underlying, condition. For example, depression resulting from a thyroid problem is best seen to by treating the thyroid problem and killing two birds with one stone. Secondary depression, though not rare, is relatively uncommon. Most cases of depression are primary, and do not derive from a pre-existing psychiatric or physical condition. If the doctor believes that your symptoms could derive from an underlying physical condition, he or she may carry out a full physical examination, obtain blood and urine samples for laboratory analysis, and perhaps arrange a brain scan.

Another of the doctor's concerns is to exclude psychiatric conditions that can be mistaken for depression. The list is fairly long, and principally includes dysthymia, adjustment disorder, bereavement, seasonal affective disorder, bipolar disorder, and a number of anxiety disorders (see later).

One of the most important and overlooked conditions that can present like depression is... none at all. The person's sadness could simply be a normal reaction to a life event or situation.

In such cases, popping a pill can do more harm than good. Antidepressants can have adverse effects. More importantly, they can lead us to think of our feelings as a medical illness rather than a reflection of real life problems that are asking to be acknowledged and addressed. At the same time, anyone going through tough times is likely to benefit from speaking to a doctor or counsellor, so, whatever the cause of your distress, don't hesitate to make contact.

Dysthymia

Dysthymia is rarely diagnosed, and is more a concept than a diagnosis. It refers to mild depressive symptoms that, though long-lasting, are not sufficiently severe to meet a diagnosis of depressive disorder.

Adjustment disorder

Adjustment disorder is a protracted response to a significant life event such as a job change, migration, or divorce. It consists of depressive symptoms and/or anxiety symptoms that are severe enough to impair social functioning, though not severe enough to warrant a diagnosis of depression or anxiety disorder. In many cases, the person feels unable to cope or carry on, and may be prone to angry outbursts. Counselling may be helpful, but adjustment disorder normally has a good outcome, resolving within a few weeks or months.

Bereavement

Bereavement refers to the grief that often occurs after the loss of a loved one, although such grief can also occur after the loss of a pet or media figure, or of an asset such as health or social status. Bereavement in such cases is normal, and varies greatly in duration and intensity from one individual to another, and, in fact, from one culture to another. Various stages or phases of bereavement have been suggested, but they are neither consistent nor universal. Sudden and unexpected loss is associated with a longer and deeper bereavement, as is the loss of someone who was very intimate or with whom one had a dependent or ambivalent relationship. A bereavement reaction might be considered abnormal if it is either unusually intense or unusually prolonged, that is, if it meets the criteria for depression or if it lasts for longer than six months. It might also be considered abnormal if it is delayed, inhibited, or distorted.

> *Dark house, by which once more I stand*
> *Here in the long unlovely street,*
> *Doors, where my heart was used to beat*
> *So quickly, waiting for a hand,*
>
> *A hand that can be clasped no more—*
> *Behold me, for I cannot sleep,*
> *And like a guilty thing I creep*
> *At earliest morning to the door.*
>
> *He is not here; but far away*
> *The noise of life begins again,*
> *And ghastly thro' the drizzling rain*
> *On the bald street breaks the blank day.*

—Alfred, Lord Tennyson, from *In Memoriam A.H.H.* (1849)

Seasonal affective disorder (SAD)

SAD is a form of depression, or depressed mood, that recurs at the same time each year. Increased sleep and carbohydrate craving are common features. SAD is thought to result from a shortening of daylight hours, and may respond to bright artificial lights given at 2500 lux in the morning and evening. There is usually complete summer remission and, occasionally, summer hypomania or mania (abnormally elevated mood, see later), which, along with Shakespeare, may be at the origin of the expression, 'This is very midsummer madness.'

Mania and bipolar disorder

Bipolar disorder (formerly 'manic-depressive illness') involves recurrent episodes of depression and mania or hypomania, interspersed with more or less lengthy periods of normal mood. The frequency, severity, and duration of the episodes are very variable, as is the proportion of depressive to manic/hypomanic episodes. Occasionally, episodes can be 'mixed', that is, feature symptoms of both depression and mania/hypomania.

In mania and hypomania, mood is markedly elated, expansive, or irritable. People with mania often dress in colourful or haphazard clothes which they complement with inappropriate accessories such as hats and sunglasses and excessive make-up, jewellery, or body art. They are hyperactive, and may come across as entertaining, charming, seductive, vigilant, assertive, bad tempered, angry, or aggressive, and sometimes all of these in turn. Thoughts race through their mind at high speed, as a consequence of which their speech is pressured and voluble and difficult to interrupt.

Sometimes, the thoughts and speech of people with mania are so muddled and rambling that they are unable to stay on topic or even make a point. They may ignore the structures and strictures of grammar, step outside the confines of the dictionary, and even talk in rhymes and puns, for example:

> They thought I was in the pantry at home... Peekaboo.... There's a magic box. Poor darling Catherine, you know, Catherine the Great, the fire grate, I'm always up the chimney. I want to scream with joy... Hallelujah!

On top of all this, mania sufferers are typically full of grandiose or unrealistic plans and projects that they begin to act upon but then quickly abandon. They often engage in impulsive and pleasure-seeking behaviours such as spending vast amounts of money, driving recklessly, taking illegal drugs, and having sex with near-strangers. As a result, they may end up harming themselves or others, running into the police and other authorities, or being exploited by the less than scrupulous.

In some cases, people with mania may experience psychotic symptoms (see Chapter 1) that make their behaviour seem all the more bizarre, irrational, and chaotic. These psychotic symptoms are usually in keeping with the elevated mood, and often involve delusions of grandeur, that is, delusions of exaggerated self-importance—of special status, special purpose, or special abilities. For instance, a mania sufferer may nurse the delusion that she is a brilliant scientist on the verge of discovering a cure for cancer, or that she is an exceptionally talented entrepreneur commissioned by her cousin the Queen to rid Africa of poverty.

People with mania invariably have poor insight into their mental state and find it difficult to accept that they are ill. This means that they are likely to delay and resist getting the help that they need, and, in the meantime, cause tremendous damage to their health, finances, careers, and relationships.

Hypomania can be thought of as a lesser degree of mania, with symptoms similar to those of mania but less severe or extreme. Mood is elated, expansive, or irritable, but, in contrast to mania, there is no marked impairment of social functioning. Some people with hypomania seem to function very effectively. But, although brimming with ideas and energy, they lack judgement and tend to make rash or risky decisions. Hypomania may or may not herald mania.

To meet the DSM-5 criteria for bipolar disorder, a person must have suffered at least one episode of abnormally elevated mood. A person who has only ever suffered depressive episodes cannot be diagnosed with bipolar disorder until and unless she has also suffered a manic or hypomanic episode. In that much, abnormally elevated mood is the hallmark of bipolar disorder.

That having been said, I should emphasize that depressive episodes in bipolar disorder can be very severe, with both psychotic symptoms and suicidal thoughts, as illustrated by this patient, who kindly agreed to relate his experience of suffering with bipolar disorder:

I have been high several times over the years, but low only once.

When I was high, I became very enthusiastic about some project or another and would work on it with determination and success. During such highs I wrote the bulk of two books and stood for parliament as an independent. I went to bed very late, if at all, and woke up very early. I didn't feel tired at all. There were times when I lost touch with reality and got carried away. At such times, I would jump from project to project without completing any, and did many things that I later regretted. Once I thought that I was Jesus and that I had a mission to save the world. It was an extremely alarming thought.

When I was low, I was an entirely different person. I felt as though life was pointless, with nothing worth living for. Although I would not have tried to end my life, I would not have regretted death. I did not have the wish or the energy to take on even the simplest task. Instead I spent my days sleeping or lying awake in bed, worrying about the financial problems that I created for myself during my highs. I also had a feeling of unreality, that people were conspiring to make life seem normal when in actual fact there was nothing there. I kept on asking the doctors and nurses to show me their ID because I just couldn't bring myself to believe that they were real.

Anxiety disorders

Anxiety can be defined as 'a state consisting of psychological and physical symptoms brought about by a sense of apprehension at a perceived threat'. Fear is similar to anxiety, except that, with fear, the threat is, or is perceived to be, more concrete, present, or imminent.

The psychological and physical symptoms of anxiety vary according to the nature and magnitude of the perceived threat, and from one person to another. Psychological symptoms may include feelings of fear and dread, an exaggerated startle reflex, poor concentration, irritability, and insomnia.

In mild to moderate anxiety, physical symptoms such as tremor, sweating, muscle tension, a faster heart rate, and faster and deeper breathing arise from the body's so-called fight-or-flight response, a state of high arousal fuelled by a surge in adrenaline.

In severe anxiety, over-breathing can lead to a fall in the concentration of carbon dioxide in the blood. This gives rise to an additional set of physical symptoms, among which chest discomfort, numbness or tingling in the hands and feet, dizziness, and faintness.

Fear and anxiety can be a normal response to life experiences, a protective mechanism that has evolved to prevent us from entering into potentially dangerous situations, and to assist us in escaping from them should they befall us regardless. For instance, anxiety can prevent us from coming into close contact with disease-carrying or poisonous animals such as rats, snakes, and spiders; from engaging with a much stronger or angrier enemy; and even from declaring our undying love to someone who is unlikely to spare our feelings. If we do find ourselves in a potentially dangerous situation, the fight-or-flight response triggered by fear can help us to mount an appropriate response by priming our body for action and increasing our performance and stamina.

In short, the purpose of fear and anxiety is to preserve us from harm, and, above all, from death—whether it be literal or metaphorical, biological or psychosocial (an idea that I develop further in Chapter 14).

Although some degree of anxiety can improve our performance on a range of tasks, severe or inappropriate anxiety can have the opposite effect and hinder our performance. Thus, whereas a confident actor may perform optimally in front of a live audience, a novice may suffer from stage fright and freeze. The relationship between anxiety and performance can be expressed graphically by a parabola or inverted 'U' (Figure 4.1).

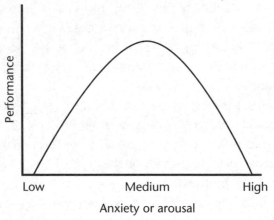

Figure 4.1: The Yerkes-Dodson curve.

According to the Yerkes-Dodson curve, a person's performance increases with arousal but only up to a certain point, beyond which it starts to decline. The Yerkes-Dodson curve best applies to complex or difficult tasks, rather than to simple tasks such as running away, for which the relationship between arousal and performance is more linear.

The Yerkes-Dodson curve indicates that very high levels of anxiety can result in handicap, even paralysis. From a medical standpoint, anxiety becomes problematic when it becomes so severe, frequent, or longstanding as to prevent us from fulfilling our occupational or social obligations. This often owes to a primary anxiety disorder, although in some instances the anxiety is secondary to another mental or physical disorder such as depression, anorexia nervosa, alcohol withdrawal, or an overactive thyroid gland.

Symptoms of anxiety are very common in depression; and, conversely, symptoms of depression are very common in anxiety disorders. The idea that anxiety and depression lie on a single spectrum of disorders is gaining ground, and the World Health Organization classification of mental disorders, the ICD-10, already contains a condition called 'mixed anxiety and depressive disorder'. This construct acknowledges that many people with depression also suffer from anxiety, either as part of the depression or in the form of a separate anxiety disorder. The relationship between depression and anxiety is a complex one, as depression can both cause and be caused by anxiety, or otherwise be associated with anxiety.

Primary anxiety disorders are very common, affecting almost one in every five people in any given year. As broadly conceived, they present in a variety of forms, including phobic anxiety disorders, panic disorder, generalized anxiety disorder, and post-traumatic stress disorder.

Phobic anxiety disorders

Phobic anxiety disorders are the most common type of anxiety disorder, and involve the persistent and irrational fear of an object, activity, or situation. Three types of phobic anxiety disorder are recognized: agoraphobia, social phobia, and specific phobia.

Contrary to popular belief, **agoraphobia** does not describe a fear of open spaces, but a fear of places that are difficult or embarrassing to escape from, typically because they are confined, crowded, or far from home. In time, people with agoraphobia may become increasingly homebound and reliant on trusted companions to accompany them on their outings.

Social phobia is the fear of being judged by others and of being embarrassed or humiliated in one or more social or performance situations such as holding a conversation or delivering a speech. Social phobia differs from normal shyness in that it starts at a later age and is more severe and debilitating, with much more prominent anxiety.

Specific phobia is by far the most common of the three phobic anxiety disorders. As its name implies, it is the fear of a specific object, activity, or situation. Common specific phobias include arachnophobia (spiders), acrophobia (heights), claustrophobia (enclosed spaces), achluophobia (darkness), brontophobia (storms), and haematophobia (blood). Unlike other anxiety disorders, specific phobias often trace their beginnings to early childhood. What's more, we seem to have a strong innate predisposition for phobias of the natural dangers commonly faced by our ancestors such as spiders and heights, even though manmade hazards such as motorcars, electric cables, and text messaging now pose much greater threats to our chances of surviving and reproducing.

Panic attacks and panic disorder

In a phobic anxiety disorder, exposure to the feared object, activity, or situation can trigger an attack of severe anxiety, or **panic attack**. During a panic attack, symptoms of anxiety are so severe that the person fears that she is suffocating, having a heart attack, losing control, or even 'going crazy'. In time, she comes to develop a fear of the panic attacks themselves, which in turn sets off further panic attacks. A vicious circle takes hold, with the panic attacks becoming ever more frequent and severe, and even occurring 'out of the blue'.

This pattern of recurrent panic attacks, called **panic disorder**, can overlie any anxiety disorder as well as depression, substance misuse, and certain physical conditions such as an overactive thyroid gland. Panic disorder often leads to so-called secondary agoraphobia, in which the person becomes increasingly home-bound to minimize the risk and consequences of further panic attacks.

Generalized anxiety disorder (GAD)

Anxiety disorders need not be specifically directed as in phobic anxiety disorders. In GAD, anxiety is not directed at any particular object, activity, or situation, but is free-floating and far-reaching. There is apprehension about a number of hypothetical events that is completely out of proportion to the actual likelihood or potential impact of those events. People with GAD fear the future to such an extent that they behave in a manner that is overly cautious and risk-averse. They are, quite literally, 'paralyzed with fear'.

Post-traumatic stress disorder (PTSD)

Anxiety related to a traumatic event can manifest in the form of PTSD. This condition was first described or recognized in the aftermath of the First World War, and its historical epithets include 'shell shock', 'combat neurosis', and 'survivor syndrome'. Common symptoms of PTSD include anxiety, of course, but also numbing, detachment, flashbacks, nightmares, partial or complete amnesia for the traumatic event, and avoidance of reminders of the traumatic event. Symptoms can last for years, and predispose to secondary mental disorders such as depression, other anxiety disorders, and alcohol dependence.

5

A philosophy of depression

Like heart disease or diabetes, depression can be highly debilitating, even fatal; but unlike heart disease or diabetes, it is poorly understood and heavily stigmatized. People with depression are often seen as failures or losers, too feeble or lazy to pick themselves up or pull themselves together.

Of course, nothing could be further from the truth. If you feel the way you do, it's most probably because you tried too hard or took on too much, so hard and so much that you made yourself ill with depression. In other words, if you feel the way you do, it is because your world was simply not good enough for you. You wanted more, you wanted better, and you wanted different, not just for yourself but for all those around you. So if you're a 'failure' or a 'loser', that's only because you set the bar much too high. You could have swept everything under the carpet and pretended, as most people do, that all is for the best in the best of worlds. But instead you had the strength and integrity to admit that something was amiss, that something was not quite right. So rather than being a failure or loser, you are all the opposite: you are ambitious, you are truthful, and you are courageous. And that is why you got ill.

But unlike heart disease or diabetes, depression can have a silver lining. Crushing though it may be, depression can present a precious opportunity to identify and address deep and difficult life problems. Just as physical pain evolved to signal injury and prevent further injury, so depression may have evolved to remove us from distressing, damaging, or futile situations. The time and space and solitude afforded by depression encourage us to reconnect with our bigger picture, and reconsider how we relate to ourselves, to others, and to the world.

In short, your depression could be your way of telling yourself that something is seriously wrong and needs working through and changing, or, at the very least, processing and understanding. Sometimes, we can become so immersed in the humdrum of our everyday lives that we no longer have the perspective or opportunity to think and feel about ourselves. The adoption of the depressive position compels us to stand back at a distance, re-evaluate and prioritize our needs, and formulate a modest but realistic plan for fulfilling them.

At an even deeper level, the adoption of the depressive position can lead us to a more refined understanding of ourselves, our lives, and life in general. From an existential standpoint, the adoption of the depressive position obliges us to become aware of our mortality and freedom, and challenges us to exercise the latter within the framework of the former. By meeting this difficult challenge, we're able to break out of the mould that has been imposed upon us, discover who we truly are, and, in so doing, begin to give deep meaning to our lives.

As stated at the beginning of Chapter 1, the concept of depression as a biological disorder may be useful for the more severe and intractable cases treated by hospital psychiatrists, but probably not for the majority of cases, which, for the most part, are mild and short-lived and more readily interpreted in terms of life circumstances, human nature, or the human condition. Thinking of unhappiness or withdrawal in terms of a mental disorder or a chemical imbalance in the brain can be counterproductive in that it can prevent us from identifying and addressing the important psychological or life problems that are at the root of our distress.

Maybe all this is more common sense than philosophy, but I do think it merits saying.

In the middle of our life's walk
I found myself alone in a dark forest
Where my path was confused.

Ah how hard it is to retell
How dense, dark, and dangerous
The thought of it alone fills me with fear!

So bitter that death is scarcely worse;
But to speak of the good I found there,
I shall tell of the other things that I saw.

—Dante, *The Divine Comedy, Hell,* opening verses

Part 2

Formal treatments

6

Talking treatments

The mystical physician said the soul was treated with
certain charms, my dear Charmides, and that these
charms were beautiful words.

—Plato, *Charmides*

Antidepressant drugs are the most readily available treatment
for depression, but, very often, psychological or so-called
talking treatments can offer a safer, more effective, and more
empowering alternative. Many people prefer talking treatments
on the grounds that they address underlying problems,
rather than merely masking superficial symptoms. Of course,
psychological treatments and drugs are not mutually exclusive,
and in some cases, such as severe psychosis, drugs may be
hard to avoid. The type of talking treatment that is chosen, if
any, depends on your symptoms and circumstances, on your
preferences, and, deplorably, on the available funding and
human resources.

Supportive therapy and counselling

At its most rudimentary, psychological treatment involves little
more than explanation, reassurance, and encouragement. Such
supportive therapy is often sorely lacking, but ought to be
offered to all people presenting with low mood. In milder cases,
supportive therapy is often the only intervention that is either
necessary or appropriate.

Counselling is similar to supportive therapy in that it involves explanation, reassurance, and encouragement. But counselling also aims at addressing life problems, and is more goal-oriented than supportive therapy.

Psychodynamic psychotherapy

In contrast to supportive therapy and counselling, exploratory psychotherapy endeavours to examine your thoughts and feelings. Two important, yet very different, forms of exploratory psychotherapy are psychodynamic psychotherapy and cognitive behavioural therapy (CBT).

Psychodynamic psychotherapy is built on the psychoanalytic theory pioneered by Sigmund Freud and others. It is similar to psychoanalysis, but briefer (a few months rather than several years) and less intensive (once a week rather than twice or thrice). Like psychoanalysis, psychodynamic psychotherapy aims to bring unconscious feelings out into the open where they can be acknowledged, experienced, and understood, and so 'dealt with'. In contrast to CBT, which is based on learning and cognitive theories, psychodynamic psychotherapy can, and usually does, delve into past and childhood experiences, and can be particularly helpful if your problems appear to be rooted there. Unfortunately, waiting times for psychodynamic psychotherapy can be several years long; if your doctor agrees that it is the best option for you, you might prefer to pay for it directly from your own pocket.

Cognitive behavioural therapy (CBT)

Developed by psychiatrist Aaron Beck in the 1960s, CBT has become a mainstream treatment for non-severe anxiety and depression as well as a number of other mental disorders. In the short-term, it is at least as effective as antidepressants, and in the longer term may be more effective at preventing relapses.

CBT is most often carried out on a one-to-one basis, but can also be delivered in small groups. It involves a set number of sessions, typically between ten and twenty, but principally takes place outside of sessions through 'homework'. You and a trained therapist (who may be a doctor, psychologist, nurse, or counsellor) develop a shared perspective on your current problems, and try to understand them in terms of your thoughts (cognitions), emotions, and behaviours, and of how these may relate to one another. This leads to the identification of realistic, time-limited goals, and of cognitive and behavioural strategies for achieving those goals.

In depression, the principal focus of CBT is on modifying automatic and self-perpetuating negative thoughts. These 'thinking errors' (Chapter 10) are considered as hypotheses which, through gentle questioning and guided discovery, can be explored, tested, and modified. Behavioural tasks might include self-monitoring, activity scheduling, graded task assignments, and assertiveness training.

CBT has garnered a great deal of institutional support on the basis that it is cheap and effective. However, critics question the robustness of the research into CBT for depression, and claim that it is in fact no more effective than other talking treatments. One particular criticism of CBT is that, by leaning so heavily on patterns of cognition, it may be mistaking the symptoms of depression for its causes while implying that depression has little or nothing to do with life circumstances. Some people can experience this reductive approach as frustrating or even alienating.

Mindfulness

Some of the concerns with CBT are addressed by mindfulness-based cognitive therapy (MBCT), which combines traditional

CBT methods with 'newer' psychological strategies such as mindfulness and mindfulness meditation.

In essence, mindfulness, which derives from Buddhist spiritual practice, aims at increasing our awareness and acceptance of incoming thoughts and feelings, and so the flexibility and fluidity of our responses, which become less like unconscious reactions and more like conscious reflections.

Mindfulness can be harnessed for the treatment of recurrent depression, stress, anxiety, and addiction, among others; but it can also be used to broadly improve the quality of our lives by decentering us and shifting our focus from doing to being.

Family therapy and interpersonal therapy (IPT)

Family therapy involves the identification and resolution of negative aspects of couple or family dynamics that may be contributing to depression, for example, deep-seated conflict, misunderstanding, or avoidance. It usually requires the direct participation of each of the parties.

Another talking treatment used in depression is **IPT**, which involves a systematic and standardized treatment approach to personal relationships and life problems contributing to depression.

If you feel that your personal relationships are eating at you, then do talk to your doctor about the possibility of counselling, family therapy, or IPT.

7

Antidepressant drugs

Fluoxetine, the first selective serotonin reuptake inhibitor (SSRI) gained regulatory approval in 1987. SSRIs are said to exert a modest antidepressant effect by preventing the reuptake of serotonin by brain cells. Compared to the older tricyclic antidepressants, they have milder adverse effects and are less toxic in overdose. Today, SSRIs such as fluoxetine, fluvoxamine, paroxetine, sertraline, and citalopram are the drugs of choice for most cases of moderate to severe depression. In fact, they have become something of a panacea, being also used in the treatment of a broad range of other mental disorders, particularly anxiety disorders, obsessive-compulsive disorder, and bulimia nervosa, and even in some physical disorders such as premature ejaculation in young men and hot flushes in menopausal women. In the UK, fluoxetine is so commonly prescribed that trace quantities have been detected in the water supply.

Since 1987, further classes of antidepressants have been developed, such as the noradrenaline reuptake inhibitors (NARIs) and the serotonin and noradrenaline reuptake inhibitors (SNRIs). These drugs are often used as second-line treatments if treatment with an SSRI has failed, but their precise role in the treatment of depression remains to be established.

Starting on an SSRI

An SSRI is normally taken once a day, in the morning. People starting on an SSRI are usually told to persist in taking their tablets because improvement in mood may be delayed for

10-20 days (in which time mood may have improved of its own accord), and because potential adverse effects are likely to be mild and short-lived. These potential adverse effects include nausea, diarrhoea, dizziness, agitation, and sexual dysfunction. With the exception of sexual dysfunction, adverse effects tend to resolve within the first month of treatment. Some SSRIs such as fluoxetine, fluvoxamine, and paroxetine inhibit certain enzymes in the liver, interfering with the breakdown of a number of drugs. If you are taking any other drugs, be sure to mention these to your prescribing doctor.

Are SSRIs dangerous?

Abruptly or rapidly stopping an SSRI can provoke a discontinuation syndrome consisting of mild and non-specific symptoms. This has led to the suggestion that SSRIs are addictive, but this is not strictly accurate in the sense that people do not get a buzz from SSRIs, and do not crave them as they might a recreational drug such as cocaine or heroin. There have also been reports that SSRIs cause, or are associated with, an increase in suicidal thoughts and behaviours in children and young people, but the studies looking into this are equivocal and the jury is still out.

How effective are SSRIs?

When I first trained in psychiatry, we used to tell patients starting on an SSRI that they had a 50–70 per cent chance of responding to their medication. However, in 2008, a paper published in the New England Journal of Medicine suggested that the effectiveness of SSRIs had been greatly exaggerated owing to a bias in the reporting of research studies. Out of 74 studies registered with the US Food and Drug Administration (FDA), 37 out of 38 studies with positive results were published in academic journals, compared to only 14 out of 36 studies with negative results. What's more, out of the 14 studies with negative results that were published, 11 were published in such a way as to convey a positive outcome. So while 94 per cent (37+11/37+14) of published studies conveyed a positive outcome, only 51 per cent (38/38+36) of all studies, published and unpublished, actually demonstrated one.

Another paper, also published in 2008, combined 35 studies submitted to the FDA before the licensing of four antidepressants including the SSRIs fluoxetine and paroxetine. The researchers found that, while the antidepressants performed better than a placebo (a dummy pill), the effect size was very small for all but very severe cases of depression.

Other drugs used in depression

If you fail to respond to your SSRI despite taking it for an adequate length of time, you and your doctor still have several pharmacological options to choose from, such as increasing the dose, trying another SSRI, or trying another antidepressant from a different class. If these options have been exhausted and time is running out, a psychiatrist might suggest adding another drug such as lithium or buspirone to 'augment' the antidepressant, although this is fairly unusual.

In the rare cases of depression with psychotic symptoms, an antipsychotic can be added to the antidepressant.

Be sure to seek your doctor's advice before coming off your medication.

St John's wort

St John's wort (*Hypericum perforatum*, Figure 7.1) is an herbal remedy that can be used in the treatment of depression. It is available over-the-counter, without the need for a medical prescription. Initial studies suggest that St John's wort is just as effective as an SSRI but with fewer adverse effects. The most common adverse effects of St John's wort are nausea, diarrhoea, dizziness, confusion, and tiredness. If you are considering an herbal remedy such as St John's wort, be sure to speak to your doctor first, particularly if you have a medical condition or allergy, if you are already on medication, or if you are pregnant or breast-feeding.

Figure 7.1:   *Hypericum perforatum* or St John's wort is a yellow-flowering perennial herb indigenous to Europe. Its common name comes from its traditional flowering and harvesting on St John's day, 24 June, when it is, or was, hung up to ward off evil.

References:
1. Turner EH et al. (2008): Selective publication of antidepressant trials and its influence on apparent efficacy. *New England Journal of Medicine* 358(3):252–60.
2. Kirsch I et al. (2008): Initial severity and antidepressant benefits: a meta-analysis of data submitted to the Food and Drug Administration. *PLoS Medicine* 5(2):e45.

8

Electroconvulsive therapy

Owing to suicidal ideation, retardation or stupor, food and drink refusal, or psychotic symptoms such as command hallucinations or nihilistic delusions, people with severe depression can pose a considerable risk to themselves. If their level of risk is very high, or if their condition has not responded to several trials of antidepressant drugs, they may be prescribed a course of electroconvulsive therapy (ECT).

A short history of ECT

It had long been known that convulsions induced by camphor could temper psychotic symptoms. In 1933, psychiatrist Manfred Sakel began using insulin injections to induce convulsions, but a period of panic and impending doom prior to convulsing made the treatment almost unbearable. Psychiatrist Ladislas Meduna replaced the insulin with a drug called metrazol, but similar problems persisted. In 1938, neuropsychiatrist Ugo Cerletti began the practice of applying a small electric shock to the head. This method, which people found more tolerable—or, rather, less intolerable—soon superseded the injections. In the 1950s, the advent of short-acting anaesthetics and muscle relaxants made it possible for patients to be put to sleep for the treatment, and dramatically reduced complications such as muscle tears and bone fractures.

How is ECT delivered?

Before starting a course of ECT, the patient should have a physical examination, a tracing of the heart (ECG), and some blood tests. She should not eat or drink from midnight on the day of treatment. In the morning, she is guided to the ECT suite. An anaesthetist gives her a standard anaesthetic and a muscle relaxant and she falls asleep. A specially trained psychiatrist then induces a seizure with a constant current, brief-pulse stimulus at a voltage that is just above her seizure threshold. The seizure typically lasts for about 30 seconds, and in many cases is so small that it cannot be seen other than on the monitor of an electroencephalogram (EEG, a device for recording the electrical activity of the brain). Most people respond to a course of between six and twelve ECT treatments, delivered over a period of three to six weeks.

Does ECT have adverse effects?

Common adverse effects of ECT include nausea, muscle aches, headache, confusion, and memory loss for events that occurred around the time of treatment and, less commonly, in the more distant past. Mortality from ECT is largely imputable to the anaesthetic, and so is comparable to that from any minor surgical procedure.

ECT and the law

In the UK, informed consent is required for ECT except if being treated under the provision of the Mental Health Act. The 2007 amendment to the Mental Health Act introduced new safeguards for the use of ECT. In short, ECT may not be imposed on a person with the capacity to refuse it, and then only if this does not conflict with any advance directive, decision of a deputy or donee, or decision of the Court of Protection.

How effective is ECT?

Opinion is divided as to the value of ECT. Several studies lend weight to the frequent anecdotal reports that ECT can be considerably more effective than antidepressant treatment.

However, opponents claim that the evidence in support of ECT is weak, and that any benefits are short-lived and outweighed by the risks, including the risk of long-term memory impairment. They also highlight that, despite decades of research, proponents of ECT cannot point, or point with certainty, to a mechanism of action for its supposed antidepressant effect.

In addition to these criticisms, ECT suffers from a poor public image. For decades, the media, including Hollywood, has mostly portrayed it as coercive, punitive, and inhumane.

There is some emerging evidence that repetitive transcranial magnetic stimulation (rTMS) could in some cases provide a safer and less off-putting alternative to ECT.

Part 3

Modular self-help

9

The 10 basic dos and don'ts of depression

If you are deep into depression and almost completely lacking in energy and motivation, a lot of the advice in this book is going to seem unrealistic. You may not even get round to reading it.

If you're going to read just one chapter, make it this one.

There are a number of simple things that anyone can do to improve their mood. You may already be doing some of these things, and you certainly don't need to be doing them all. Just do the ones that you feel most comfortable with, or that are easiest for you. As your mood begins to lift—and, believe me, sooner or later it will—you can make more and bigger changes to your routine. If you can hold on to these good habits once your mood has lifted, you will not only be feeling better, but better than ever before.

1. **Spend more time with sympathetic friends and relatives**. Talking to others about our feelings helps us to process them, put them into perspective, and obtain advice and support. Don't be afraid to tell people that you need their help, or feel guilty for accepting it. If you feel uncomfortable talking to friends and relatives, or are unable to, you can phone one of the helplines listed at the back of this book. Perhaps you prefer not to talk about your feelings. Even so, spending time with sympathetic people and doing things together should help to lift your mood.

2. **Don't bite off more than you can chew**: break down large tasks into smaller ones, and set yourself realistic deadlines for completing them. Try to reduce your stress (Chapter 12). Don't blame yourself for 'doing nothing': you are merely giving yourself the time and space that you need to get better. Just think of it as taking a step back to jump further.

3. **Spend more time doing the things that you normally enjoy**, even if they no longer seem so appealing: read your favourite childhood book, go to the shops or cinema, prepare a meal, spend time with an old friend—anything that gets you out of yourself and takes your mind off negative thoughts is likely to make things better.

4. **Get out of the house**, even if only to buy a pint of milk or walk in the park. Bright daylight, fresh air, and the hustle bustle of everyday life can all be very helpful, as can the sights, sounds, and smells of nature. If you can, try to take some mild exercise, such as 20 minutes of brisk walking.

5. **Fight off negative thoughts**. Make a list of all the positive things about yourself and your situation (you may need help with this), keep it on you, and read it several times a day. However bad you may be feeling, remember that you have not always felt this way, and will not always feel this way.

6. **Be realistic about your progress**: improvements in mood are likely to be gradual rather than sudden, and you may even get worse before you start getting better. Once you are on the right track, there are going to be bad days as well as good days (Figure 9.1). Bad days that come after one or several good days may seem all the worse for it. Don't blame yourself for the bad days, and don't despair.

7. **Avoid making or acting upon important decisions** such as leaving your job, getting divorced, or spending a large amount of money. While in the throes of depression, thinking errors (Chapter 10) are likely to impair your judgement.

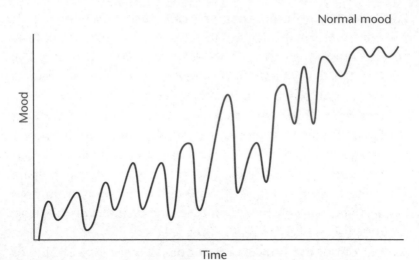

Figure 9.1: Improvements in mood are likely to be gradual rather than sudden, and there are going to be bad days as well as good days.

8. **Get as much sleep as you can**. A single good night's sleep, or even a nice nap, can make a world of difference to your mood. To sleep better and longer, follow some of the tips in Chapter 23.

9. **Make an appointment with a health professional** such as your family doctor, psychiatrist, or key worker, and enlist their advice and support. Maybe ask for some counselling and take things from there.

10. **Decide whom to call in an emergency** should you feel overwhelmed by negative or suicidal thoughts. This may be a relative or friend, your key worker, or a helpline. Think of a backup in case you can't get hold of your primary support. Carry the appropriate telephone numbers on your person at all times, for example, on your phone or in your wallet.

10

Correcting thinking errors

Thinking errors, also called cognitive distortions or cognitive biases, are irrational patterns of thinking that can both cause depression, and be caused by depression: the more depressed you feel, the more you are bugged by thinking errors, and the more you are bugged by thinking errors, the more depressed you feel.

To break this vicious circle, you need to identify your thinking errors and successfully challenge them. You may need help with this, so maybe ask a trusted friend or relative to read this chapter and discuss it with you.

Seven common thinking errors in depression are:

1. **Arbitrary inference**: drawing a conclusion in the absence of supporting evidence. For example,

   The whole world hates me.

   Questions to challenge arbitrary inference:
   Why do I say that?
   Why would that be the case?
   Can I think of anything that goes against this statement?
   Is anyone else in the same predicament?

2. **Over-generalization**: drawing a conclusion on the basis of very limited evidence. For example,

   My sister did not come to visit me. The whole world hates me.

   Questions to challenge over-generalization:
   Could there be other ways of explaining my evidence?
   Is my evidence strong enough to warrant that conclusion?

Is my conclusion too broad?
Can I think of anything that goes against my conclusion?

3. **Magnification and minimization**: over- or under-estimating the importance or significance of an event. For example,

Now that my cat is dead, I'll never have anything to look forward to.

Questions to challenge magnification and minimization:
Has this ever happened to me before? How did I cope?
How would other people cope in a similar situation?
What are some of the other good things in my life?
Am I seeing this in the right perspective?

4. **Selective abstraction**: focusing on a single negative event or condition to the exclusion of other, more positive ones. For example,

The nurse hates me. She gave me an annoyed look three days ago. (But never mind that she spent an hour with me this morning.)

Questions to challenge selective abstraction:
Why would this be the case?
Am I looking at all the evidence?
Are there some more positive things that I can focus on?
What are other people telling me?

5. **Dichotomous thinking**: 'all or nothing' or 'black and white' thinking. For example,

If he doesn't come to see me today, then he doesn't love me.

Questions to challenge dichotomous thinking:
Could there be any other reasons? (What else could have held him back?)
Does it have to mean that?
Is it really all black and white? Or could there be shades of grey?
Can I think of anything that goes against my conclusion?

6. **Personalization**: relating independent events to oneself. For example,

The nurse went on holiday because she was fed up with me.

Questions to challenge personalization:
   Are there any other possible explanations?
   Is my explanation the most likely explanation?
   What evidence do I have for this?
   Am I reading too much into things?

7. **Catastrophic thinking**: exaggerating the consequences of an event or situation. For example,

The pain in my knee is getting worse. When I'm reduced to a wheelchair, I won't be able to go to work and pay the mortgage. So I'll end up losing my house and dying in the street.

Questions to challenge catastrophic thinking:
   Are things as bad as they could be?
   What is the most likely outcome?
   What action can I take to prevent this outcome?
   Could any good come out of this situation?

11

Depressive realism

While it is true that people who are low in mood can suffer from grave thinking errors (Chapter 10), the scientific literature suggests that those with only mild to moderate depression can also have more accurate judgement about the outcome of so-called contingent events (events which may or may not occur), and a more realistic perception of their social role, abilities, and possibilities.

This so-called 'depressive realism' may enable people who are low in mood to cast off the Polyannish optimism and rose-tinted spectacles that shield us from reality, to see life more accurately, and to judge it accordingly.

If so, the concept of depression may—at least in some cases—be turned on its head and positively redefined as something like 'the healthy suspicion that modern life has no meaning and that modern society is absurd and alienating'.

For many health experts, this is the sort of irreligion that calls for anathema. Yet the question of the meaning of life is the most important that a person can ask, and the realization that life might or should be lived differently, and the difficult challenges that this poses, are bound to provoke a depressive reaction, a harsh winter that opens out onto a beautiful spring.

We must be careful not to confuse our human nature with inadequacy, or the tender shoots of wisdom with mental disorder.

12

Managing stress

Stress is an important cause of depression (Chapter 3). Although stress is often related to life events such as losing a loved one, getting divorced, or falling ill, most of the day-to-day stress that we experience comes from smaller 'background' stressors such as constant deadlines, tense relationships, painful memories, isolation, discrimination, poor housing, and unpaid bills.

The amount of stress that a person can handle is largely related to her thinking styles and social skills. People with positive thinking styles and good social skills are in a better position to diffuse stressful situations—for example, by doing something about them, putting them into perspective, or talking through them with someone.

1. The first step in dealing with stress is to **recognize its warning signs**. Study Table 12.1 and write down how you feel when you become stressed.
2. Next, make a list of situations in which you feel that way.
3. For each situation on your list, come up with one or more strategies for preventing, avoiding, or diffusing it. See Figure 12.1 for an example of such a list.

You can also use some more general strategies for reducing stress.

Deep breathing involves regulating your breathing:

- Breathe in through your nose and hold the air in for several seconds.
- Then purse your lips and gradually let the air out. Let out as much air as you can.
- Carry on until you feel more relaxed.

You can combine deep breathing with **relaxation exercises**:

– Lying on your back, tighten the muscles in your toes for 10 seconds and then relax them completely.
– Do the same for your feet, ankles, and calves, working up all the way to your head and neck.

Table 12.1: Common symptoms of stress

Emotional symptoms	Anxiety, fear, irritability, anger, resentment, loss of confidence
Cognitive symptoms	Difficulty concentrating or making decisions, confusion, repetitive or circular thoughts
Physical symptoms	Dry mouth, tremor, sweatiness, pounding or racing heartbeat, chest tightness and difficulty breathing, muscle tension, headache, dizziness
Behavioural symptoms	Nervous habits such as nail biting or pacing, drinking more coffee and alcohol, eating too much or too little, sleeping poorly, acting brashly or unreasonably, losing your temper, being inconsiderate to others, neglecting your responsibilities

List of stressful situations

Arguing with Liz	★ Talk to Liz about how I'm feeling and try to sort things out with her ★ See her less often ★ Avoid talking to her about certain things ★ Walk away from arguments ★ Use deep breathing
Receiving bills I can't pay	★ Ask Stan to help me with my finances ★ Speak to a social worker to see what help I can get ★ Phone the bank to try to reach an agreement

Figure 12.1: Make a list of situations that stress you out. For each situation on your list, come up with one or more strategies for preventing, avoiding, or diffusing it.

Other general strategies for reducing stress include listening to music, particularly classical music like Bach or Chopin, taking a hot bath, reading a book or surfing the internet, calling or meeting up with a friend, practising yoga or meditation, and playing sports.

Lifestyle changes can assist both to reduce stress and to increase your resilience to stress. Lifestyle changes to consider include:

- Simplifying your life, even if this means doing less or doing only one thing at a time.
- Drawing up a schedule and sticking to it.
- Getting enough sleep.
- Exercising regularly (for example, walking, swimming, yoga...)
- Having, or giving, a massage.
- Eating a balanced diet.
- Restricting your intake of coffee.
- Restricting your intake of alcohol.
- Taking time out to do the things you enjoy.
- Connecting with others by sharing thoughts and feelings.
- Altering your thinking styles: be more realistic, reframe problems, test your thoughts and feelings, and maintain a sense of humour.

These lifestyle changes are useful not only for reducing stress, but also for improving your overall health and quality of life. Though individually small and simple, their cumulative effect can be absolutely transformative.

If you continue to struggle with stress, discuss the issue with a health professional and ask for relaxation training.

13

Managing anxiety

The first step in managing your anxiety is to learn as much as you can about it (Chapter 4).

It can be tempting to avoid the objects or situations that make you anxious, but in the long term such avoidance behaviour is counterproductive. When anxiety comes, repress the urge to escape. Instead, accept your anxiety and wait for it to pass. Easier said than done, of course, but it's important that you try.

Breaking down the problem

One effective method for specific anxiety (anxiety related to a specific object or situation) is to break the problem down into a series of tasks, rank the tasks in order of difficulty, and start on the easiest task. For example, a person with arachnophobia may first think about spiders, then look at pictures of spiders, and then look at real spiders from a safe distance, and so on. Return to the easiest task day after day until you feel fairly comfortable with it. Give yourself as long as you need, then move on to the next easiest task and repeat. Try to be positive: although the symptoms of anxiety can be terrifying, they cannot actually harm you.

Relaxation techniques

If a particular task or situation is very anxiety provoking, use relaxation techniques to manage your anxiety. These techniques are very similar to those used to manage stress (Chapter 12), and can also be used for generalized anxiety, that is, free-floating anxiety that is not tied to any particular object or situation.

One common and effective strategy, called **deep breathing**, involves modifying and regulating your breathing:

- Breathe in through your nose and hold the air in for several seconds.
- Then purse your lips and gradually let the air out. Let out as much air as you can.
- Carry on until you feel more relaxed.

You can combine deep breathing with **relaxation exercises:**

- Lying on your back, tighten the muscles in your toes for 10 seconds and then relax them completely.
- Do the same for your feet, ankles, and calves, working up all the way to your head and neck.

Other strategies

General strategies, including lifestyle changes, for coping with anxiety are the same as those for reducing stress, and are listed in Chapter 12 on managing stress. Stress and anxiety often go hand in hand, and reducing the one should also reduce the other.

Getting help

If, despite implementing some of these strategies, you are still crippled with anxiety, get in touch with a charity such as Anxiety UK which offers different types of support, including self-help groups.

You can also speak to your doctor who may refer you for a talking treatment or perhaps recommend that you start on an antidepressant (Chapter 7, antidepressants are also used in the treatment of anxiety). Medication, if prescribed, is usually most effective if combined with a talking treatment, most commonly cognitive-behavioural therapy (CBT, Chapter 6).

If your anxiety is extremely severe, your doctor may offer to prescribe a benzodiazepine sedative. Such sedatives are not a cure for anxiety, but can provide short-term relief from certain symptoms. Sedatives should only be taken for short periods because their long-term use leads to tolerance (needing more and more to produce the same effect) and dependence/addiction.

Your doctor might also or instead recommend propranolol or another beta-blocker drug to control specific symptoms such as palpitations associated with a fast heart rate. Beta-blockers should be avoided in certain groups, most notably people with a history of asthma or heart problems.

14

A philosophical cure for anxiety

The psychologist Abraham Maslow proposed that healthy human beings have certain needs, and that these needs are arranged in a hierarchy, with some needs (such as physiological and safety needs) being more primitive or basic than others (such as social and ego needs). Maslow's so-called 'hierarchy of needs' is often presented as a five-level pyramid (Figure 14.1), with higher needs coming into focus only once lower, more basic needs have been met.

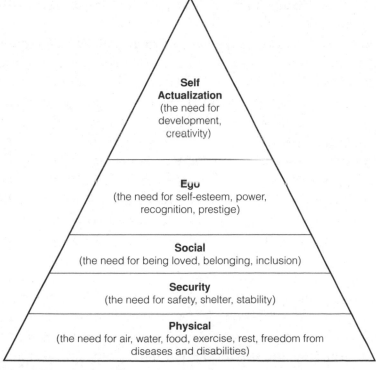

Self Actualization
(the need for development, creativity)

Ego
(the need for self-esteem, power, recognition, prestige)

Social
(the need for being loved, belonging, inclusion)

Security
(the need for safety, shelter, stability)

Physical
(the need for air, water, food, exercise, rest, freedom from diseases and disabilities)

Figure 14.1: Maslow's hierarchy of needs.

Maslow called the inferior levels of the pyramid 'deficiency needs' because we do not feel anything if they are met, but become anxious or distressed if they are not. Thus, physiological needs such as eating, drinking, and sleeping are deficiency needs, as are safety needs, social needs such as friendship and sexual intimacy, and ego needs such as self-esteem and recognition. On the other hand, he called the fifth, top level of the pyramid a 'growth need' because our need to self-actualize enables us to fulfil our true and highest potential as human beings.

Once we have met our deficiency needs, the focus of our anxiety shifts to self-actualization, and we begin, even if only at a sub- or semi-conscious level, to contemplate our bigger picture. However, only a minority of people are able to self-actualize because self-actualization calls for uncommon qualities such as honesty, independence, awareness, objectivity, creativity, and originality.

Many people who have met all their deficiency needs do not self-actualize, instead inventing more deficiency needs for themselves—because to contemplate the meaning of their life and of life in general would lead them to entertain the possibility of their meaninglessness and the prospect of their own death and annihilation.

A person who begins to contemplate his bigger picture may come to fear that life is meaningless and death inevitable, but at the same time cling on to the cherished belief that her life is eternal or important or at least significant. This gives rise to an inner conflict that is sometimes referred to as 'existential anxiety' or, more colourfully, 'the trauma of non-being'.

While fear and anxiety and their pathological forms (such as agoraphobia or panic disorder) are grounded in threats to life (Chapter 4), existential anxiety is rooted in the brevity and apparent meaninglessness or absurdity of life. Existential anxiety is so disturbing and unsettling that most people avoid it at all costs, constructing a false reality out of goals, ambitions, habits, customs, values, culture, and religion to deceive themselves that their lives are special and meaningful and that death is distant or delusory.

Unfortunately, such self-deception comes at a significant price. According to philosopher Jean-Paul Sartre, people who refuse to face up to 'non-being' are acting in 'bad faith', and living out a life that is inauthentic and unfulfilling. Facing up to non-being can bring insecurity, loneliness, responsibility, and consequently anxiety, but it can also bring a sense of calm, freedom, and even nobility. Far from being pathological, existential anxiety is a sign of health, strength, and courage, and a harbinger of bigger and better things to come.

For theologian Paul Tillich, refusing to face up to non-being leads not only to a life that is inauthentic but also to pathological (or neurotic) anxiety. In *The Courage To Be*, Tillich asserts:

> *He who does not succeed in taking his anxiety courageously upon himself can succeed in avoiding the extreme situation of despair by escaping into neurosis. He still affirms himself but on a limited scale. Neurosis is the way of avoiding non-being by avoiding being.*

According to this startling outlook, pathological anxiety, though seemingly grounded in threats to life, in fact arises from repressed existential anxiety, which itself arises from our uniquely human capacity for self-consciousness.

Facing up to non-being enables us to put our life into perspective, see it in its entirety, and thereby lend it a sense of direction and unity. If the ultimate source of anxiety is fear of the future, the future ends in death; and if the ultimate source of anxiety is uncertainty, death is the only certainty. It is only by facing up to death, accepting its inevitably, and integrating it into life that we can escape from the pettiness and paralysis of anxiety, and, in so doing, free ourselves to make the most out of our lives and ourselves.

15

The search for meaning

Ever more people today have the means to live, but no meaning to live for.

—Victor Frankl

In *Man's Search for Meaning*, psychiatrist Victor Frankl wrote about his ordeal as a concentration camp inmate during the Second World War. Interestingly, he found that those who survived longest in concentration camps were not those who were physically strong, but those who retained a sense of control over their environment. He observed:

> *We who lived in concentration camps can remember the men who walked through the huts comforting others, giving away their last piece of bread. They may have been few in number, but they offer sufficient proof that everything can be taken from a man but one thing: the last of human freedoms—to choose one's own attitude in any given set of circumstances—to choose one's own way.*

Frankl's message is ultimately one of hope: even in the most absurd, painful, and dehumanizing of circumstances, life can be given a meaning, and so too can suffering. Life in the concentration camp taught Frankl that our main drive or motivation in life is neither pleasure, as Freud had believed, nor power, as Adler had believed, but meaning.

After his release, Frankl founded the school of logotherapy (from the Greek *logos*, meaning 'reason' or 'principle'), which is sometimes referred to as the 'Third Viennese School of Psychotherapy' for coming after those of Freud and Adler. The aim of logotherapy is to carry out an existential analysis of the person, and, in so doing, to help her uncover or discover meaning for her life.

According to Frankl, meaning can be found through:

- Experiencing reality by interacting authentically with the environment and with others,
- Giving something back to the world through creativity and self-expression, and
- Changing our attitude when faced with a situation or circumstance that we cannot change.

Frankl is credited with coining the term 'Sunday neurosis' to refer to the dejection that many people feel at the end of the working week when at last they have the time to realize just how empty and meaningless their life has become. This existential vacuum may open the door on all sorts of excesses and compensations such as neurotic anxiety, avoidance, binge eating, drinking, overworking, and overspending. In the short-term, these excesses and compensations carpet over the existential vacuum, but in the longer term they prevent action from being taken and meaning from being found.

For Frankl, depression results when the gap between what a person is and what he ought to be, or once wished to be, becomes so large that it can no longer be carpeted over. The person's goals seem far out of reach and he can no longer envision a future. As in Psalm 41, *abyssus abyssum invocat*—'hell brings forth hell', or, in an alternative translation, 'the deep calls unto the deep'.

Under this light, depression is our way of telling ourselves that something needs to change. Unless change can be made, there will continue to be a mismatch between our lived experience and our desired experience, between the meaninglessness of everyday life and the innate drive to find meaning, to self-actualize, to be all that we can be. Those who have a 'why' to live, said Frankl, can bear with almost any 'how'.

16

The happiness trap

In the past 60 or 70 years, real term incomes in countries such as the US and UK have increased dramatically, but happiness has not kept apace. In fact, people today are considerably less happy than back then: they have less time, they are more alone, and so many of their number are on antidepressants that trace quantities have been detected in the water supply.

Although economists focus on the absolute size of salaries, several sociological studies have found that the effect of money on happiness results less from the things that money can buy (absolute income effect) than from comparing one's income to that of others, and in particular one's peers (relative income effect). This is an important part of the explanation as to why people today are no happier than 60 or 70 years ago: despite being considerably richer and healthier, they have barely been able to 'keep up with the Joneses', who now, along with the rich and famous, constantly flaunt themselves on social media.

But there is more. If I am to believe everything that I see in the mass media, happiness is to be six foot tall or more and to have bleached teeth and a firm abdomen, all the latest clothes, accessories, and electronics, a picture-perfect partner who is both a great lover and a terrific friend, an assortment of healthy and happy children, a large house in the right sort of neighbourhood, a second property in an idyllic holiday location, a top-of-the-range car to shuttle back and forth from the one to the other, a clique of friends with whom to have fabulous dinner parties, three or four foreign holidays a year, and a high-impact job that does not distract from any of the above.

There are at least three major problems that I can see with this ideal of happiness. First, it represents a state of affairs that is impossible to attain to and therefore in itself an important source of unhappiness. Second, it is situated in an idealized and hypothetical future rather than in an imperfect but actual present in which true happiness is much more likely to be found, albeit with a great deal of thought and effort. Third, and most importantly, it has largely been defined by commercial interests that have absolutely nothing to do with true happiness, which has far more to do with the practice of reason and the perspective and awareness that this gradually brings.

In short, it is not just that the bar for happiness is set too high, but also that it is set in the wrong place, and that it is, in fact, the wrong bar. Jump and you'll only break your back.

17

The philosophy of happiness

In his famous *Nicomachean Ethics*, the philosopher Aristotle tries to discover what is 'the supreme good for man', by which he means the best way to lead our life and give it meaning. For Aristotle, a thing is best understood by looking at its end, purpose, or goal. For example, the purpose of a knife is to cut, and it is by seeing this that one best understands what a knife is; the goal of medicine is good health, and it is by seeing this that one best understands what medicine is.

Now, if one carries on with this for some time, it soon becomes apparent that some goals are subordinate to other goals, which are themselves subordinate to yet other goals. For instance, a medical student's goal may be to qualify as a doctor, but this goal is subordinate to his goal to heal the sick, which is itself subordinate to his goal to make a living by doing something useful. This could go on and on, but unless the medical student has a goal that is an end-in-itself, nothing that he does is actually worth doing. What, asks Aristotle, is this terminal goal? This 'supreme good', says Aristotle, is happiness.

> *And of this nature happiness is mostly thought to be, for this we choose always for its own sake, and never with a view to anything further: whereas honour, pleasure, intellect, in fact every excellence we choose for their own sakes, it is true, but we choose them also with a view to happiness, conceiving that through their instrumentality we shall be happy: but no man chooses happiness with a view to them, nor in fact with a view to any other thing whatsoever.*

But what exactly is happiness? Recall that, for Aristotle, it is by understanding the distinctive function of a thing that one can understand its essence. Thus, one cannot understand what it is to be a gardener unless one can understand that the distinctive function of a gardener is 'to tend to a garden with a certain degree of skill'. Whereas human beings need nourishment like plants and have sentience like animals, their distinctive function, says Aristotle, is their unique capacity to reason. Thus, our supreme good, or happiness, is to lead a life that enables us to deploy and develop our reason, and that is in accordance with rational principles. Unlike amusement or pleasure, which can also be enjoyed by animals, happiness is not a state but an activity, and it is profound and enduring.

Aristotle acknowledges that our good or bad fortune can play a part in determining our happiness; for example, he acknowledges that happiness can be affected by such factors as our material circumstances, our place in society, and even our looks. Yet he maintains that by living our life to the full according to our essential nature as rational beings, we are bound to become happy regardless. For this reason, happiness is more a question of behaviour and of habit—of virtue—than of luck; a person who cultivates such behaviours and habits is able to bear his misfortunes with equanimity, and thus can never be said to be truly unhappy.

18

Practising phenomenology

The hardest thing to see is what is in front of your eyes.

—Goethe

Phenomena derives from the Ancient Greek meaning 'things that appear', and the practice of phenomenology can be defined as the direct examination and description of phenomena as they are consciously experienced.

Pioneered by the philosopher Edmund Husserl (1859-1938), phenomenology involves paying close attention to objects and their relations so that they begin to reveal themselves, not as we take them to be, but as they truly appear to naked human consciousness, shorn of superimposed theories, preconceptions, abstractions, interpretations, and emotional associations.

Unlike other philosophical approaches, phenomenology is not a theory or set of theories, but a formal method for accessing bare human experience as it unfolds, moment by moment. It enables us to study not only the phenomena themselves, but also, by extension, the very structures of human experience and consciousness.

Phenomenology is not quite synonymous with mindfulness. Mindfulness, which derives from Buddhist spiritual practice, aims at increasing our awareness and acceptance of incoming thoughts and feelings, and so the flexibility or fluidity of our responses, which become less like unconscious reactions and more like conscious reflections. Phenomenology, in contrast, is more explicitly outward-looking.

Phenomenological activities such as writing, drawing, painting, gardening, bird watching, and wine tasting remove us from our tired and tortured heads and return us to the world that we came from, reconnecting us with something much greater and higher than our personal problems and preoccupations. **Phenomenology can, quite literally, bring us back to life.** In his book *The Philosophy of Existence* (1938), the psychiatrist and philosopher Karl Theodor Jaspers described phenomenology as 'a thinking that, in knowing, reminds me, awakens me, brings me to myself, transforms me'. To describe is to know, to know is to understand, and to understand is to own, enjoy, and, to some extent, control. Like mindfulness, phenomenology is a balm not only for depression, anxiety, and stress, but also for boredom, loneliness, greed, selfishness, apathy, alienation, and any number of human ills.

Figure 18.1: The miracle of a robin on a garden fence. Vision, said the painter James Ensor, changes while it observes.

If that were not enough, phenomenological practice offers a number of other benefits and advantages.

Wine tasters, for example, often say that blind tasting (tasting a wine without knowing its identity) enables them to:

- Set a standard of objectivity
- Test, stretch, and develop their senses
- Apply their judgement
- Recall old memories
- Compare their analysis with that of their peers
- Discuss the wine and learn about it, and about wine in general
- Forge meaningful human relationships, and
- Imbibe the wine with the respect and consideration that it deserves.

In refining their senses and aesthetic judgement, wine tasters become much more conscious of the richness not only of wine but also of other potentially complex beverages such as tea, coffee, and spirits, and by extension, the aromas and flavours in food, the scents in the air, and the play of light in the world.

For life is consciousness, and consciousness is life.

19

The psychology of boredom

The modern concept of boredom goes back to the 19th century. For Erich Fromm and other thinkers, boredom was a response to industrial society in which people are required to engage in alienated labour, and to the erosion of traditional structures of meaning. Yet, it seems that boredom of some form is a human universal. On the walls of the ruins of Pompeii, there is Latin graffiti about boredom that dates back to the first century.

Boredom can be defined as a profoundly unpleasant state of unmet arousal: you are aroused rather than despondent, but, for one or more reasons, your arousal cannot be met or directed. These reasons can be internal—often a lack of imagination, motivation, or concentration—or external, such as an absence of environmental stimuli or opportunities. So while we want to do something more stimulating, we find ourselves unable to do so; moreover, we are frustrated by the rising awareness of this inability. Awareness, or consciousness, is key, and may explain why animals, if they get bored at all, generally have much higher thresholds for boredom.

Boredom is often brought about or aggravated by a lack of control or freedom, which is why it is particularly common in children and teenagers, who, in addition to being shepherded, lack the resources to escape from boredom.

For the gloomy philosopher Arthur Schopenhauer, boredom is evidence of the meaninglessness of life; because, if life were intrinsically meaningful or fulfilling there could be no such thing as boredom. Boredom opens the shutters on some very uncomfortable thoughts and feelings, which we normally block out by keeping busy. This is the essence of the manic defence, which consists in preventing feelings of helplessness and despair from entering our conscious mind by occupying it with opposite feelings of euphoria, purposeful activity, and omnipotent control—we are, in the words of Virginia Woolf, 'always giving parties to cover the silence'.

Boredom is so unpleasant that we expend considerable energy and resources on preventing or reducing it. The value of the global entertainment industry topped $2 trillion in 2016, and entertainers and athletes are accorded extravagantly high levels of pay and social status. The technological advances of recent years have put an eternity of entertainment at our fingertips, but, paradoxically, this has only made things worse, in part, by removing us even further from reality. Instead of being satiated, we are desensitized and in need of ever more stimulation, ever more war, gore, and hardcore.

What we tend to neglect is that boredom also has its benefits. Boredom serves as a signal that we're not spending our time as well as we could, that we should rather be doing something more enjoyable, more useful, more important, or more fulfilling. And so boredom can be a stimulus for change, leading us on to better ideas, higher ambitions, and greater opportunities. Most of our achievements, of man's achievements, are born out of the dread of boredom.

There are many ways of reducing our propensity to boredom. If boredom is an awareness of unmet arousal, we can minimize boredom by avoiding situations over which we have no or little control, cutting out distractions, motivating ourselves, putting things into their proper perspective (realizing how lucky we really are), expecting less, and so on.

But rather than fight a constant battle against boredom, it is easier and much more productive to actually embrace it. If boredom is a window on the fundamental nature of reality, and, by extension, on the human condition, then fighting boredom amounts to pulling the curtains. Yes, the night outside is pitch black, but the stars shine all the more brightly for it. For just these reasons, many Eastern traditions embrace and encourage boredom, seeing it as the pathway to a higher consciousness.

So instead of fighting boredom, go along with it, make something out of it; in short, be yourself less boring. Schopenhauer said that boredom is but the reverse side of fascination, since both depend on being outside rather than inside a situation, and one leads to the other. So instead of being outside a situation, get inside it, however hard this may seem. The Buddhist monk Thich Nhat Hanh advocates appending the word 'meditation' to whatever activity it is that you find boring, for example, 'waiting in an airport—meditation'. In the words of the writer Samuel Johnson, 'It is by studying little things that we attain the great art of having as little misery and as much happiness as possible.'

20

The Buddhist angle

At the heart of Buddhist philosophy is the idea that our very concept of the self is something of an illusion. The term *anattā* refers to the 'not-self', which is composed of five *skandhas* or elements, namely, body, sensation, perception, will, and consciousness. These five *skandhas* are in a constant state of flux, but create for the not-self the illusion of continuity, that is, the illusion of self. This explains why if you try to become conscious of yourself, you will only ever become conscious of such and such feeling, such and such perception, or such and such thought, but never of an actual, core self.

In Buddhist thought, the death of the bodily self leads to the disaggregation of the *skandhas* and to their re-aggregation into another self which is neither identical to nor entirely different from the previous self, but which forms part of a continuum with it. An analogy that is often used to describe this process of rebirth or *samsāra* is that of a flame passing from one candle to the next.

This cycle of rebirth can only ever be broken if the empirical, changing self is able to transcend its subjective distorted image of the world, which is both conscious and unconscious, and which has the 'I am' conceit at its heart. This, then, is heaven or *nirvana*. Nirvana, as I see it, rests on the understanding that consciousness is a sequence of moments rather than the continuity of the 'I am' conceit. Each moment is an experience of an individual mind-state such as a perception, feeling, or thought; the consciousness of an empirical self is made up of the birth and death of these individual mind-states, and 'rebirth' is nothing more than the persistence of this process beyond 'our' 'death'.

Immersing ourselves in the present moment to escape, even if for a short time, from the 'I am' conceit can provide some much needed relief from negative thoughts and feelings. As with phenomenology (Chapter 18), our shifted state and perception can bring us calm and perspective, and raise our spirits.

21

The psychology of gratitude

*I would maintain that thanks are the highest form of
thought, and that gratitude is happiness doubled by wonder.*

—GK Chesterton

Gratitude never came easily to us men and women, and is a diminishing virtue in modern times. In our consumerist society, we tend to focus on what we lack, or on what other people have that we do not, whereas gratitude is the feeling of appreciation for what we already have. More than that, gratitude is the recognition that the good in our life can come from something that is outside us and outside our control, and that owes little or nothing to us.

By turning us outward, gratitude shifts our focus from what we lack or strive for to what we already have, opening our eyes to the bounty that is life, something to marvel at, revel in, and celebrate rather than forget, ignore, or take for granted as it flies us by. This much broader perspective frees us to live life, no longer for our narrow selves, but for life itself.

The ancient philosopher Cicero called gratitude the mother of all the other virtues, and modern science has begun to catch up with him. Studies have linked gratitude with increased satisfaction, motivation, and energy; better sleep and health; and reduced stress and sadness. Grateful people are much more engaged with their environment, leading to greater personal growth and self-acceptance, and stronger feelings of purpose, meaning, and specialness.

Despite these many and varied benefits, gratitude is hard to cultivate. It opposes itself to some deeply ingrained human traits such as our striving to better our lot, our need to feel in control of our destiny, and our propensity to credit ourselves for our successes while blaming others for our failures. As human nature does not leave much place for it, gratitude is an attainment of maturity, or, to be more precise, emotional maturity. Children taught to parrot 'thank you' rarely mean it, and even as adults we often make a superficial display of gratitude because that is the 'done thing'. Gratitude is good manners, and good manners aim at aping profundity when profundity is lacking.

Real gratitude, in contrast, is a rare virtue. There is a fable in Aesop about a slave who pulls a thorn out of the paw of a lion. Some time later, the slave and the lion are captured, and the slave is thrown to the lion. The starved lion rushes bounding and roaring toward the slave, but upon recognizing his friend fawns upon him and licks his hands and face like a puppy dog.

'Gratitude', concludes Aesop, 'is the sign of noble souls.'

Like all virtues, gratitude requires constant cultivation, until such a day as we can say, 'Thank you for nothing.'

22

Chicken soup for the soul

Chicken soup (or, to be technically precise, chicken broth or *bouillon*) is a great dish: simple, healthy, comforting, and ever so delicious, to say nothing of the therapeutic value that simple everyday activities like cooking can have in terms of empowerment, self-affirmation, and self-expression, and of reconnecting us with others and the world around us. The only common adverse effect is the washing up afterwards!

A soup should be much more than a bunch of chopped up ingredients floating about in a dilute liquid. Instead, it should be a subtle, balanced, and yet concentrated infusion of those ingredients. To get there, you need to simmer over a low heat, not just cook as fast as possible. You are aiming for nothing less than the holy trinity of chicken soup: a bright colour, a marbled patina, and for the steaming flesh to fall off the bone and melt in the mouth.

Ingredients for two

– The best chicken thighs and/or drumsticks that you can find, ideally from hens that have had a good life. Four pieces.
– Two or three leeks, finely chopped.
– A little bit of celery and carrot, finely diced (optional).
– A home-made *bouquet garni* consisting of a small handful of parsley, a few sprigs of thyme, and three or four bay leaves, all tied together in a bundle.
– Chicken or vegetable stock. 1.5 litres.
– Some butter and/or olive oil.

- A few pinches of sea salt and freshly ground black pepper.
- A loaf of bread.

Instructions

- Melt the butter in a large pan. Add in some olive oil to stop the butter from burning. Brown the chicken until the skin is a rich golden colour. This gives the soup much more flavour.
- Add the chopped leeks and any other vegetables.
- Add the stock and top up with some water if need be.
- Add the *bouquet garni*.
- Add some salt and pepper. Don't overdo the salt, as the stock will already be quite salty.
- Simmer under a lid for about one hour.
- Discard the *bouquet garni*.
- Adjust the salt and pepper.
- Decorate with some fresh parsley—or not.
- Serve with bread and enjoy!
- If you want to have some wine with the soup, try a buttery Chardonnay.

23

Better sleep in 10 simple steps

Methought I heard a voice cry 'Sleep no more!
Macbeth doth murder sleep', the innocent sleep,
Sleep that knits up the ravell'd sleeve of care,
The death of each day's life, sore labour's bath,
Balm of hurt minds, great nature's second course,
Chief nourisher in life's feast.

—Shakespeare, Macbeth

Insomnia—difficulty in falling or staying asleep—affects as many as 1 in 3 people, and almost anyone could do with better, more restorative sleep. Insomnia usually becomes a problem if it occurs on most nights and causes distress or daytime effects such as fatigue, poor concentration, and irritability.

The relationship between insomnia and depression is far from simple, as insomnia can both cause and be caused by depression. Insomnia not only predisposes to depression but also exacerbates existing depressive symptoms, making it harder to pull through. Insomnia also predisposes to other mental disorders such as anxiety disorders and psychotic disorders; to physical problems such as infections, high blood pressure, obesity, and diabetes; and to motoring and other accidents.

Aside from depression, common causes or contributors to insomnia include poor sleeping habits, other mental disorders such as anxiety disorders and psychotic disorders, physical problems such as pain or shortness of breath, certain prescription medications, and alcohol and drug misuse.

The most important causes of short-term insomnia (the commonest type of insomnia) are a stressful life event, a poor sleeping environment, and an irregular routine.

If you are suffering from insomnia, there are a number of simple measures that you can take to resolve or at least reduce the problem:

1. **Set up a strict routine** involving regular and adequate sleeping times (most adults need about seven or eight hours sleep every night). Allocate a time for sleeping, for example, 11pm to 7am, and don't use this time for anything else. Avoid daytime naps, or make them short and regular. If you have a bad night, avoid sleeping late, as this makes it more difficult to fall asleep the following night.

2. **Devise a relaxing bedtime routine** that enables you to wind down before bedtime. This may involve breathing exercises or meditation or simply reading a book, listening to music, or watching TV.

3. **Enjoy a hot, non-caffeinated drink** such as herbal tea or hot chocolate. In time, your hot drink could become a sleeping cue.

4. **Sleep in a familiar, dark, and quiet room** that is adequately ventilated and neither too hot nor too cold. Try to use this room for sleeping only, so that you come to associate it with sleep. In time, your room could become another sleeping cue.

5. **If sleep doesn't come, don't become anxious or annoyed** and try to force yourself to sleep. The more aggravated you become, the less likely you are to fall asleep. Instead, try to clear your mind and relax. For example, I find that making myself feel grateful for something soon sends me off to sleep. Alternatively, get up and do something relaxing and enjoyable for about half an hour before giving it another go.

6. **Exercise regularly**. This will also help you with your low mood (Chapter 24). However, don't workout too close to

bedtime as the short-term alerting effects of exercise may make it harder to fall asleep.

7. **Reduce your overall stress** (Chapter 12). At the same time, try to do something productive or enjoyable each day. As da Vinci said, a well-spent day brings happy sleep (and a well-spent life brings happy death).

8. **Eat a wholesome evening meal** with a good balance of protein and complex carbohydrates. Eating too much can make it difficult to fall asleep; eating too little can disturb your sleep and decrease its quality.

9. **Avoid caffeine, alcohol, and tobacco**, particularly in the evening. Alcohol may make you fall asleep more readily, but it decreases the overall length and quality of your sleep.

10. **If insomnia persists despite these measures, speak to your doctor**. In some cases, insomnia has a very specific cause such as a physical problem or an adverse effect of your medication that requires your doctor's attention.

Other interventions

Behavioural interventions such as sleep restriction therapy or cognitive-behavioural therapy can be helpful in some cases and are preferable to sleeping tablets in the long-term.

Sleeping tablets can be effective in the short-term, but are best avoided in the longer term because of their adverse effects and high potential for tolerance (needing more and more to produce the same effect) and dependence/addiction.

Retail, over-the-counter sleeping remedies often contain an antihistamine that can leave you feeling drowsy the following morning. If you decide to use such remedies, be sure not to drive or operate heavy machinery the next day.

Herbal alternatives are usually based on valerian, a hardy perennial flowering plant with heads of sweetly scented pink or white flowers. If you are considering a herbal remedy, do speak to your doctor, particularly if you're already on medication, or are pregnant or breast-feeding.

Figure 23.1:   Valerian flowerheads.

24

Releasing endorphins

Regular exercise sustains both physical and mental health.

With regard to physical health, exercise helps us to become, or remain, slim and toned. It decreases blood pressure and heart rate, increases physical strength and endurance, and improves posture and flexibility. It also improves sleep and appetite, which in depression can be severely disturbed.

With regard to psychological health, exercise decreases stress, improves concentration and memory, boosts self-esteem, and directly lifts mood through the release of natural antidepressants called endorphins. By getting you out of the house and 'out of yourself', exercise can remove you from emotional conflict, distract you from your symptoms, and increase the frequency of your social interactions. It also gives you something to look forward to, and something by which to structure your day and regulate your body clock.

Exercise doesn't have to be demanding: 15 or 30 minutes of moderate activity a day is a very good start, and if you make it regular it starts to feel easier. You could do some gardening, walk in the park, cycle to the shops, join classes at the gym or swimming pool, get involved in a team sports, install an exercise bike or cross trainer in front of your television, or just dance around the living room. Dancing, if you can manage it, can be remarkably uplifting, and also enables you to express yourself. The possibilities are such that you are bound to find something to suit your interests and current levels of motivation. But be careful not to push yourself too hard, or you may end up feeling worse.

Other ways to give your endorphins a boost include: holding someone's hand, giving and receiving massage, having a hot bath, laughing, singing, lighting a scented candle, and enjoying a delicious meal.

25

Coping with psychotic symptoms

A substantial minority of people with severe depression also suffer from psychotic symptoms, that is, hallucinations and/or delusions.

As discussed in Chapter 1, the most common hallucinations are auditory, involving voices and sounds. Voices are often mocking or attacking, seeking to undermine the person, and may goad the person into harming herself. Voices can be highly distressing, especially if they involve threats or abuse, or if they are loud and incessant.

Delusions in depression are commonly along the themes of guilt or poverty. Delusions of guilt involve the belief that one has committed a crime or sinned greatly, while delusions of poverty involve the belief that one is being, or has been, ruined. Delusions can also take on 'nihilistic' overtones. *Nihil* is Latin for 'nothing', and nihilistic delusions involve the belief that one is about to be reduced to nothing, that is, to die or suffer a personal catastrophe, or even that one is already dead.

For obvious reasons, there is little in the way of self-help that sufferers can do to address their delusions—other, of course, than engaging with their carers, care team, and treatment plan (see below).

But there are some simple measures that anyone can take to reduce or eliminate auditory hallucinations. If you're assailed by voices, try out some of the following things:

- Keep a diary of the voices to help identify and avoid the situations in which they arise.
- Identify a trusted person with whom to discuss the voices.

- Focus your attention on a distraction activity such as reading, gardening, singing, or listening to music.
- Talk back to the voices: challenge them and insist that they go away.
- Manage your levels of stress and anxiety (Chapters 12 and 13).
- Improve your sleeping habits (Chapter 23).
- Avoid alcohol and recreational drugs (Chapter 26).
- Take your medication as prescribed.

Advice for carers

Psychotic symptoms can also be extremely distressing to carers. Carers typically find themselves challenging their loved one's delusions and hallucinations, partly out of a desire to relieve her suffering, and partly out of understandable feelings of fear and helplessness. Unfortunately, this can be counterproductive, because it can alienate the depression sufferer at the very time when she is most in need of care. Difficult though this is, carers should remind themselves that their loved one's experiences are as real to her as they are unreal to everyone else.

A much more constructive/less confrontational approach for carers is to recognize that their loved one's psychotic symptoms are important to her, while making it clear that they themselves do not personally share in them.

For example:

- The devil told me that I'm to blame for everything that's happened.
- Are you hearing him now?
- No, he's just stopped talking.
- What else did he say?
- That I'm a very bad person and don't deserve to be looked after.

- Has he been telling you to harm yourself?
- No, he hasn't, although I sometimes feel as though I should.
- Would you actually harm yourself?
- No, no, of course not.
- Gosh, this all sounds terrifying. How are you feeling?
- I've never felt so frightened in all my life.
- I do understand that, although I myself have never heard the devil you speak of.
- Didn't you hear him earlier on?
- No, not at all. I've never heard or seen him.
- What about all the evil spirits?
- No, I haven't heard them either, not at all. Have you tried ignoring all these voices?
- If I listen to my iPod they don't seem so loud, and I can actually hear myself think.
- What about when we talk together, like now?
- Yes, that's very helpful too. I feel much less frightened now.

26

Coming off alcohol and drugs

People with depression who drink heavily or use drugs such as cannabis, cocaine, and heroin are very likely to delay their recovery, and, beyond that, to suffer more frequent and severe relapses in their illness.

People with depression often turn to alcohol and drugs to relieve their symptoms. These substances may temporarily blunt or mask their symptoms, but in the longer term make them much worse. A vicious circle takes hold: the more a person uses substances, the worse her symptoms become; and the worse they become, the more she uses substances.

What's more, alcohol and drug use may prevent people with depression from obtaining and engaging with the support that they need.

Other possible consequences of substance use include:

– Family and marital difficulties. Substance use can be very hard on a partner or spouse.
– Motoring offences.
– Accidents.
– Unemployment.
– Financial hardship.
– Criminal activity and its consequences.
– Increased likelihood (and severity) of psychotic symptoms.
– Malnutrition.
– Poor compliance with prescribed medication.
– Physical complications such as high blood pressure, heart attacks, stroke, stomach ulcers, and liver disease.

- Complications of intravenous drug use such as hepatitis, HIV, and venous thrombosis.
- Death by accidental overdose.

Advice and support are readily available from your doctor or care worker. Ask a health professional to help you draw up a plan to come clean. Tasks in this plan could in the first instance include keeping a diary of your substance use, taking your medication as prescribed, and attending scheduled appointments. Relatives and friends can play an important role in supporting and monitoring your progress, and, if possible, should be included in your plan. Substance use is often prompted by stressful situations, so learning about techniques for managing stress and anxiety such as deep breathing (Chapters 12 and 13) can be very helpful, as can role-playing specific social skills that you can then deploy in high-risk situations. These social skills might include going into a pub and ordering a non-alcoholic drink, or saying 'no' to a drug dealer. If you find yourself in a high-risk situation and are about to cave in, call a friend, relative, or helpline, discuss your thoughts and feelings, and get the support that you need to pull through. You can find wider support in local support groups, or in more structured 12 step programmes such as Alcoholics Anonymous or Narcotics Anonymous. There are also other options and interventions, including detoxification if you have reached the stage of dependence. Be sure to talk things through carefully with your doctor or care worker. The first step is usually the hardest one.

27

Fighting thoughts of self-harm

Acts of self-harm such as self-cutting or overdosing may be carried out for a variety of reasons, most commonly to express or relieve bottled-up anger or tension, feel more in control of a seemingly desperate life situation, or punish oneself for being a 'bad' person.

For some people, the pain inflicted by self-harm is preferable to the numbness and emptiness that it replaces: it is something rather than nothing, and a salutary reminder that one is still able to feel, that one is still alive. For others, the pain of self-harm merely replaces a different kind of pain that they can neither understand nor control.

Acts of self-harm reflect deep distress, and are most often used as a desperate and reluctant last resort—a means of surviving rather than dying, and sometimes also a means of attracting much-needed attention and support.

For many people, self-harm is a one-off response to a severe emotional crisis. For others, it is a more long-term issue. People may carry on self-harming because they carry on suffering from the same problems, or they may stop self-harming for a time, perhaps several years, only to return to it at the next major emotional crisis.

Practical advice

If you are plagued by thoughts of self-harm, there are several coping strategies that you can use.

An effective coping strategy is to find someone that you trust, such as a friend, relative, or teacher, and share your feelings with him or her. If you can't find anyone, or there is no one you feel comfortable sharing your feelings with, there are a number of helplines listed at the back of this book that you can ring at any time of day or night.

Engaging in creative activities such as writing, drawing, or playing a musical instrument can distract you from the urge to self-harm, and also enable you to express and understand your feelings. Other distraction techniques include reading a good book, listening to music, watching a comedy or nature programme, or even just going out to the shops. Relaxation techniques like deep breathing (Chapter 12) can also help, as can yoga and meditation. However, avoid alcohol and drugs (Chapter 26) as these can make your behaviour much more impulsive and dangerous.

In some cases, the urge to self-harm may be so great that all you can do is minimize the risks involved. Things to try: hold ice cubes in your palm and attempt to crush them, fit an elastic band around your wrist and flick it, or pluck off the hairs on your arms and legs.

If you have harmed yourself and are in pain or unable to stop the bleeding, or if you have taken an overdose of whatever type or size, get someone to take you to A&E as soon as possible or call emergency services.

Once things are more settled, consider asking for a talking treatment such as counselling or cognitive behavioural therapy. Joining a local support group enables you to meet people with similar problems, that is, people who are likely to accept and understand you, and with whom you may feel more comfortable sharing your thoughts, feelings, and experiences. However, beware of unmonitored online forums and chat groups, which are open to all and sundry, including trolls, and can leave you feeling even worse.

28

Fighting suicidal thoughts

If you are assailed by suicidal thoughts, remember that most people who have attempted suicide and survived ultimately feel relieved that they did not end their life.

Some of the thoughts you may be having include:

- I want to escape my suffering.
- I have no other options.
- I'm a horrible person and don't deserve to live.
- I've betrayed those I love.
- Those I love would be better off without me.
- I want someone/people to know how bad I'm feeling.
- I want someone/people to know how bad they've made me feel.

Whatever thoughts are running through your mind, and however terrible you're feeling, remember that you have not always felt this way, and that you will not always feel this way.

The risk of a person committing suicide is highest in the combined presence of (1) suicidal thoughts, (2) the means to commit suicide, and (3) the opportunity to commit suicide. If you're prone to suicidal thoughts, ensure that any means of committing suicide have been removed. For example, give tablets and sharp objects to a trusted person for safekeeping, or put them in a locked or otherwise inaccessible place. Also ensure that the opportunity to commit suicide is lacking by remaining in close contact with one or more people, for instance, by inviting them to stay over or going to stay with them. Share your thoughts and feelings with these people, and don't be reluctant to let them help you. If no one is available or no one seems suitable, there are a number of helplines listed at the back of this book that you can ring at any time of day or night. You can even take yourself to A&E or ring for an ambulance.

Do not use alcohol or drugs as these can make your behaviour more impulsive and significantly increase your likelihood of doing something dangerous. In particular, don't drink or take drugs when alone, or when you're going to end up alone.

Make a list of all the positive things about yourself and all the positive things about your life, including the things that have so far kept you from ending it (you may need help with this). Keep the lists on you, and read them to yourself whenever you are assailed by suicidal thoughts.

On a separate sheet of paper, write a safety plan for the times when you feel like acting on your suicidal thoughts. Your safety plan could involve delaying any suicide attempt by at least 48 hours, and, in the meanwhile, talking to a trusted person about your thoughts and feelings. Discuss your safety plan with a health professional and commit yourself to it.

My safety plan

• Read through the list of positive things about myself.	• Delay any suicidal attempt by at least 48 hours.
• Read through the list of positive things about my life and remind myself of the things that have so far prevented me from committing suicide.	• Call Stan on (phone number). If he is unreachable, call Julia on (phone number). Or call my care worker on (phone number), or the crisis line on (phone number).
• Distract myself from suicidal thoughts by reading a book, listening to jazz, or watching my favourite film or comedy.	• Go to a place where I feel safe such as the sports or community centre.
• Get a good night's sleep. Take a sleeping tablet if necessary.	• Go to A&E. • Call for an ambulance.

Figure 28.1:   Example of a safety plan.

Sometimes, even a single night's sleep can completely change our outlook, and sleep is also an escape from suicidal thoughts and associated feelings. If you're sleeping badly or not enough, follow some of the advice in Chapter 23.

Once things are a bit more settled, try to address the cause or causes of your suicidal thoughts in as far as possible. Discuss this with your doctor, care worker, or another health professional.

29

A King Solomon legend

Once upon a time, King Solomon decided to humble his most powerful minister. "Benaiah," he boomed, wearing his sternest face, "I want you to search high and low and find for me a special ring." "Your Majesty, yes, of course. What ring would that be?" "It is a magical ring," said Solomon, "which makes its bearer sad if he is happy and happy if he is sad. I want to wear it for Sukkot, which gives you six months to find it."

Benaiah searched every street in the city, both within and without the walls, and every town and village for miles around. He rode into far-flung provinces and foreign lands with bags of gold under his cloak, but no one could sell him the magic ring. No one had even heard of it.

The faithful chief minister returned crestfallen to Jerusalem. He crept through the east gate and was wending his way to the royal palace when a ragged merchant beckoned him. "Sire," said the gnarled old man, "the city speaks of nothing but your quest, and I, though very humble, believe that I have the treasure for which you seek." The old man produced a plain gold band on which he proceeded to engrave three letters. When Benaiah saw the engraving, he thanked the old man with all the gold that he was carrying.

That night, a great feast was held for Sukkot, with the finest dishes and richest wines. "Well, my dear Benaiah, have you found the ring?" Solomon grinned from ear to ear; behind him, his other ministers snickered. But to their astonishment, Benaiah pulled out a ring and, holding it with both hands, presented it to Solomon. As Solomon examined the ring, a great black cloud fell upon him, and, sensing the change in mood, the ministers fell silent. On the gold band the old man had engraved the letters Gimel, Zayin, and Yud, which begin the words *Gam zeh ya'avor*— This too shall pass.

30

The philosophy of suicide

The Church has long argued that one's life is the property of God and thus that to commit suicide is to deride God's prerogatives. The counterargument, by the philosopher David Hume, is that, if such is the case, then to save someone's life is also to deride God's prerogatives.

Most religions share the Church's belief in the sanctity of life, although a few have come to regard at least some suicides as honourable. For example, a number of Tibetan monks have killed themselves to protest the Chinese occupation of Tibet—although this is perhaps more a case of self-sacrifice than suicide proper.

Legal systems have historically been informed by religion, such that in many jurisdictions suicide and attempted suicide are still illegal. The very expression 'commit suicide' implies a crime or sin. In the UK, the Suicide Act of 1961 decriminalized suicide and attempted suicide.

Unlike most people, some philosophers prefer to think of suicide less in terms of ethics and more in terms of a finely balanced calculation. But the reality is that the vast majority of suicides are not the product of cool-headed deliberation, the so-called 'rational suicide', but of uncontrollable anguish and despair.

Regardless of the morality or permissibility of committing suicide, suicide entails death, and so the question naturally arises as to whether death should or should not be feared. In his influential paper of 1970, tersely entitled *Death*, the philosopher Thomas Nagel addresses precisely this question: if death is the permanent end of our existence, is it an evil?

Either death is an evil because it deprives us of life, or it is a mere blank because there is no one left to experience this deprivation. Thus, if death is an evil, this is not in virtue of any positive attribute that it has, but in virtue of what it deprives us from, namely, life. For Nagel, the bare experience of life is intrinsically valuable, regardless of the balance of its good and bad elements.

The longer we are alive, the more we 'accumulate' life. In contrast, death cannot be accumulated—it is not 'an evil of which Shakespeare has so far received a larger portion than Proust'. Most people would not consider the temporary suspension of life as an evil, nor would they regard the long period before they were born as an evil. Therefore, if death is an evil this is not because it involves a period of non-existence, but because it deprives us of life.

Nagel draws three objections to this view, but only so as to later counter them. First, it is doubtful whether anything can be an evil unless it actually causes displeasure. Second, in the case of death there is no subject left on whom to impute an evil. As long as we exist, we have not yet died; and once we have died, we no longer exist. So there seems to be no time at which we might suffer the evil of death. Third, if most people would not regard the long period before they were born as an evil, then why should they regard the period after they are dead any differently?

Nagel counters these three objections by arguing that the good or evil that befalls us depends on our history and possibilities rather than on our momentary state, such that an evil can befall us even if we are not here to experience it. For instance, if an intelligent person receives a head injury that reduces her mental condition to that of a contented infant, this should be considered a serious evil even if the person herself (in her current state) is oblivious to her fate.

Thus, if the three objections are invalid, it is essentially because they ignore the direction of time. Even though we cannot survive our death, we can still suffer evil; and even though we do not exist during the time before our birth and the time after our death, the time after our death is time of which we have been deprived, time in which we could have carried on enjoying the good of living.

The question remains as to whether the non-realization of further life is an absolute evil, or whether this depends on what can naturally be hoped for: the death of Keats at 24 is commonly regarded as tragic, but that of Tolstoy at 82 is not.

'The trouble,' says Nagel, 'is that life familiarizes us with the goods of which death deprives us... Death, no matter how inevitable, is an abrupt cancellation of indefinitely extensive goods.'

31

The philosophy of hope

Hope is a desire for something combined with an anticipation of it happening, it is the anticipation of something desired. To hope for something is to make a claim about something's significance to us, and so to make a claim about ourselves.

One opposite of hope is fear, which is the desire for something not to happen combined with an anticipation of it happening. Inherent in every hope is a fear, and in every fear a hope. Other opposites of hope are hopelessness and despair, which is an agitated form of hopelessness.

Hope is often symbolized by harbingers of spring such as the swallow, and there is a saying that 'there is no life without hope'. Hope is an expression of confidence in life, and the basis for more practical dispositions such as patience, determination, and courage. It provides us not only with aims, but also with the motivation to attain those aims. As the theologian Martin Luther said, 'Everything that is done in the world is done by hope.' Hope not only looks to the future but also makes present hardship easier to bear, sustaining us through our winters.

At a deeper level, hope links our present to our past and future, providing us with an overarching narrative that lends shape and meaning to our life. Our hopes are the strands that run through our life, defining our struggles, our successes and setbacks, our strengths and shortcomings, and in some sense enobling them. Running with this idea, our hopes, though profoundly human—because only humans can project themselves into the distant future—also connect us with something much greater than ourselves, a cosmic life force that moves in us as it does in all of nature. Conversely, hopelessness is both a cause and a symptom of depression, and, within the context of depression, a strong predictor of suicide. "What do you hope for out of life?" is one of my most important questions as a psychiatrist, and if my patient replies "nothing" I have to take that very seriously.

Hope is pleasant in so far as the anticipation of a desire is pleasant. But hope is also painful, because the desired circumstance is not yet at hand, and, moreover, may never be at hand. Whereas realistic or reasonable hopes are more likely to lift us up and move us on, false hopes are more likely to prolong our torment, leading to inevitable frustration, disappointment, and resentment. The pain of harbouring hopes, and the greater pain of having them dashed, explains why most people tend to be modest in their hoping.

In his essay of 1942, *The Myth of Sisyphus*, the philosopher Albert Camus compares the human condition to the plight of Sisyphus, a mythological king of Ephyra who was punished for his chronic deceitfulness by being made to repeat forever the same meaningless task of pushing a boulder up a mountain, only to see it roll back down again. Camus concludes, 'The struggle to the top is itself enough to fill a man's heart. One must imagine Sisyphus happy.'

Even in a state of utter hopelessness, Sisyphus can still be happy. Indeed, he is happy precisely because he is in a state of utter hopelessness, because in recognizing and accepting the hopelessness of his condition, he at the same time transcends it.

32

Building relationships

A man is happy if he has merely encountered the shadow of a friend.

—Menander

Building quality relationships is particularly important for people who suffer with low mood. Strong, healthy relationships can provide you with vital practical and emotional support. Talking things through enables you to share the pain, solve problems, and test your perspective. More generally, spending time with others can pull you out of yourself, lift your mood, and boost your self-esteem.

The first rule of building relationships is to be authentic. Don't try to be who you imagine people would like you to be. By being yourself from the very start, you can quickly and instinctively gauge whether you feel comfortable with someone. Instead of focusing your attention on playing a part, focus it on nurturing each other and enjoying each other's company.

Of course, no one is perfect, and you may need to make allowances for people's shortcomings, just as you might expect them to make allowances for yours. Bear in mind that, in some cases, a person's 'faults' may simply reflect different backgrounds and perspectives. Try to respect people's differences, to value them, and to learn and grow from them. Remember that, like authenticity, respect is usually reciprocated: the more you give, the more you receive in return.

In any relationship, tensions and conflicts are bound to arise. These are often silent and unspoken, and it's important to develop a sort of instinct for them. If you sense some friction and are bothered by it, bring this up at the soonest opportunity. Gently and gradually explain your thoughts and feelings. Be sure to listen to the other person's point of view and check that there have not been any misunderstandings. Don't assume that the other person knows what you expect, and be very clear about what this is. At the same time, be prepared to negotiate and compromise. The best outcome is usually that which satisfies both parties, although in some cases it may be politic for the one or the other to give way. Relationships should be mutually supportive, and being supportive, particularly when we are the weaker party, can be extremely rewarding.

33

Dealing with insults and put-downs

Insults can be physical, such as punching, slapping, or spitting. More usually, they are verbal, whether direct or indirect. Examples of indirect verbal insults are jokes and ironic comments, backhanded compliments, mimicry, and false fascination. Ocular and facial expressions can substitute for speech: a cold or constant stare, a false or exaggerated smile, or a raised eyebrow can, depending on their intention, also count as indirect verbal insults.

All of the above involve actively doing something, and count as insults of commission. But insults of omission are equally if not more common. Examples of insults of omission (assuming that they aren't genuine omissions) are not inviting or including someone, not deferring to her age or rank, and not responding to her friendly gestures, including basic eye contact.

So, what is the best way of dealing with all these insults?

1. Anger.

This is the weakest possible response, and this for three main reasons. First, it shows that we take the insult, and therefore the insulter, seriously. Second, it suggests that there is truth in the insult. And third, it upsets and abases us—which can invite further insults.

2. Acceptance

This may seem like a very weak response, but, in some cases, can be the strongest response of all. When someone insults us, we ought to consider three things: whether the insult is true, who it came from, and why. If the insult is true or largely true, the person it came from is reasonable, and her motive is worthy, then the insult is not an insult but a statement of fact and, what's more, one that is potentially very helpful to us. Thus, we seldom take offence at our teacher, parent, or best friend.

In general, if you respect the person who insulted you, you ought to give thought to the insult and learn as much as you can from it. On the other hand, if you think that the person who insulted you is unworthy of your consideration, you have no reason to take offence, just as you have no reason to take offence at a naughty child or barking dog. **So whatever the case, you have no reason to take offence.**

3. Returning the insult

There are several problems with the put-down, even if it is a very clever one. First, it does have to be clever, and, second, it has to occur to us at just the right moment. But even if we are as razor sharp as Oscar Wilde, a witty put-down is unlikely to be our best defence. The problem with the put-down, however witty it may be, is that it tends to equalize us with our insulter, raising her up to our level and bringing us down to hers. This gives her and her insult much too much credibility. The witty put-down should only be used among friends, and only to add to the merriment. And it should be followed by something like a toast or a pat on the shoulder. In other words, it should only be used for the purposes of humour.

4. Humour

Humour is an especially effective response for three reasons: it undermines the insult, it brings the audience (if any) on side, and it diffuses the tension of the situation. Cato the Younger, the Roman statesman and stoic philosopher, was pleading a case when his adversary Lentulus spat in his face. After wiping off the spittle, Cato said, 'I will swear to anyone, Lentulus, that people are wrong to say that you cannot use your mouth.'

Sometimes, it might even be appropriate to exaggerate or add to the insult so as to make a mockery of the insulter and, by extension, the insult: "Ah, if only you had known me better, you would have found greater fault still!"

5. Ignoring the insult

One downside of humour is that it requires quick thinking. Ignoring the insult is easier and, in fact, more powerful. One day, a boor struck Cato at the public baths. When the boor realized that it was Cato whom he had struck, he came to apologize. Instead of getting angry or accepting his apology, Cato replied, 'I don't remember being struck.' Subtext: 'You are so insignificant that I don't even care to register your apology, let alone take offence at your insult.'

In conclusion

In conclusion, we need never take offence at an insult. Offence exists not in the insult but in our reaction to it, and our reactions are completely within our control. It is unreasonable to expect a boor to be anything but a boor; if we take offence at her bad behaviour, we have only ourselves to blame.

Acknowledgement: The principal ideas and examples in this chapter are from *A Guide to the Good Life: The Ancient Art of Stoic Joy* by William Irvine.

34

The 7 types of love

Most of us seem to be hankering after romantic love, but few of us realize that, far from being timeless and universal, romantic love is in fact a modern construct that emerged in tandem with the novel.

In *Madame Bovary* (1856), itself a novel, Gustave Flaubert tells us that Emma Bovary only found out about romantic love through 'the refuse of old lending libraries'. These books, he writes:

> ...were all about love and lovers, damsels in distress swooning in lonely lodges, postillions slaughtered all along the road, horses ridden to death on every page, gloomy forests, troubles of the heart, vows, sobs, tears, kisses, rowing-boats in the moonlight, nightingales in the grove, gentlemen brave as lions and gentle as lambs, too virtuous to be true, invariably well-dressed, and weeping like fountains.

There are, of course, many other ways to love, not all of which are compatible with romantic love. By preoccupying ourselves with romantic love, we risk neglecting other types of love that are more readily accessible and may, especially in the longer term, prove more healing and fulfilling.

The seven types of love discussed below are loosely based on classical readings, especially of Plato and Aristotle, and on J. A. Lee's 1973 book, *Colours of Love*.

1. Eros

Eros is sexual or passionate love, and is the type most akin to the modern construct of romantic love. In Greek myth, it is a form of madness brought about by one of Cupid's arrows. The arrow breaches us and we 'fall' in love, as did Paris with Helen, leading to the Trojan War and destruction of Troy. In more modern times, eros has been amalgamated with the broader life force or will, a fundamentally blind process of striving for survival and reproduction. Eros has also been contrasted with Logos, or Reason, with Cupid depicted as a blindfolded child.

2. Philia

The hallmark of philia, or friendship, is shared goodwill. The philosopher Aristotle believed a person can bear goodwill to another for one of three reasons: that she is useful; that she is pleasant; and, above all, that she is good, that is, rational and virtuous. Friendships founded on goodness are associated not only with mutual benefit but also with companionship, dependability, and trust.

3. Storge

Storge ('stor-gae'), or familial love, is a kind of philia pertaining to the love between parents and their children. It differs from most philia in that it tends, especially with younger children, to be unilateral or asymmetrical. More broadly, storge is the fondness born out of familiarity or dependency. Unlike eros or philia, it does not hang on our personal qualities. People in the early stages of a romantic relationship often expect unconditional storge, but find only eros, and, if they are lucky, philia. Over time, eros often mutates into storge, and, if we are lucky, there is philia and pragma (see below) as well.

4. Agape

Agape is universal love, such as the love for strangers, nature, or God. Unlike storge, it does not depend on filiation or familiarity. Also called charity by Christian thinkers, agape encompasses the modern concept of altruism, defined as unselfish concern for the welfare of others. Recent studies link altruism to a number of benefits. In the short term, altruism leaves us with a euphoric feeling—the so-called 'helper's high'. In the longer term, it is associated with better mental and physical health, as well as longevity. More generally, altruism, or agape, helps to build and maintain the psychological, social, and, indeed, environmental fabric that shields, sustains, and enriches us. Given the increasing anger and division in our society, and the state of our planet, we could all do with quite a lot more agape!

5. Ludus

Ludus is playful or uncommitted love. It can involve activities such as teasing and dancing, or more overt flirting, seducing, and conjugating. The focus is on fun, and sometimes on conquest, with no strings attached. Ludic relationships are easy-going, undemanding, and uncomplicated but, for all that, can be long-lasting. Ludus works best when both parties are self-sufficient. Problems arise when one party mistakes ludus for eros, whereas ludus is in fact much more compatible with philia.

6. Pragma

Pragma is a kind of practical love founded on reason or duty and one's longer term interests. Sexual attraction takes a back seat in favour of personal qualities and compatibilities, shared goals, and 'making it work'. In the days of arranged marriages, pragma must have been extremely common. Although unfashionable, it remains widespread, most visibly in certain high-profile celebrity and political pairings. Pragma may seem opposed to ludus, but the two can co-exist, with the one providing a counterpoint to the other. In the best of cases, the partners in the pragma relationship agree to turn a blind eye or even, as in the case of Simone de Beauvoir and Jean-Paul Sartre, a sympathetic eye.

7. Philautia

Philautia is self-love, which can be healthy or unhealthy. Healthy self-love is akin to self-esteem, which is our cognitive and, above all, emotional appraisal of our own worth. More than that, it is the matrix through which we think, feel, and act, and reflects and determines our relation to ourselves, to others, and to the world. Self-esteem and self-confidence do not always go hand in hand. In particular, it is possible to be highly self-confident and yet to have profoundly low self-esteem, as is the case with many performers and celebrities.

People with high self-esteem do not need to prop themselves up with externals such as income, status, or notoriety, or lean on crutches such as alcohol, drugs, or sex. They are able to invest themselves fully in projects and people because they do not fear failure or rejection. Of course they suffer hurt and disappointment, but their setbacks neither damage nor diminish them. Owing to their resilience, they are open to growth experiences and relationships, tolerant of risk, quick to joy and delight, and accepting and forgiving of themselves and others.

In conclusion

Of course, there is a kind of porosity between the seven types of love, which keep on seeping and passing into one another. For Plato, love aims at beautiful and good things, because the possession of beautiful and good things is called happiness. Of all beautiful and good things, the best, most beautiful, and most dependable is truth or wisdom, which is why Plato called love not a god but a philosopher:

He whom love touches not walks in darkness.

35

Building self-esteem

Low self-esteem can be deeply rooted, with origins in traumatic childhood experiences such as prolonged separation from parent figures, neglect, or emotional, physical, or sexual abuse. In later life, self-esteem can be undermined by ill health, negative life events such as losing a job or getting divorced, deficient or frustrating relationships, and a general sense of lack of control. This sense of lack of control may be especially marked in victims of emotional, physical, or sexual abuse, or victims of discrimination on the grounds of religion, culture, race, sex, or sexual orientation.

The relationship between low self-esteem and mental disorder and mental distress is very complex. Low self-esteem predisposes to mental disorder, which in turn knocks self-esteem. In some cases, low self-esteem is in itself a cardinal feature of mental disorder—as, of course, in depression.

People with low self-esteem tend to see the world as a hostile place and themselves as its victims. As a result, they are reluctant to express and assert themselves, miss out on experiences and opportunities, and feel powerless to change things. All this lowers their self-esteem still further, sucking them into a vicious circle.

If you feel that you suffer from poor self-esteem, there are a number of simple things that you can do to boost yourself and, hopefully, break out of the downward spiral. You may already be doing some of these things, and you certainly don't need to do them all. Just do the ones that you feel most comfortable with.

1. **Make two lists: one of your strengths and one of your achievements.** Try to get a supportive friend or relative to help you with these lists, as people with low mood are not usually in the most objective frame of mind. Keep the lists in a safe place and read through them every morning.

2. **Think more positively about yourself.** Remind yourself that, despite your problems, you are a unique, special, and valuable person, and that you deserve to feel good about yourself. You are, after all, a miracle of consciousness, the consciousness of the universe. Identify and challenge any negative thoughts about yourself such as 'I'm a loser', 'I never do anything right', and 'No one really likes me'.

3. **Pay special attention to your personal hygiene:** take a shower, brush your hair, trim your nails, and so on.

4. **Wear clean, well-fitting clothes that make you feel good about yourself.** All things being equal, wear an ironed shirt instead of a crumpled T-shirt. You get the idea…

5. **Eat good food as part of a healthy, balanced diet.** Make meals a special time, even if you are eating alone. Turn off the TV, set the table, light a candle, and make a moment to feel grateful (Chapter 21).

6. **Exercise regularly** (Chapter 24). Go for a brisk walk every day, even if it is cold or rainy, and take more vigorous exercise (exercise that makes you sweat) two or three times a week.

7. **Ensure that you're getting enough sleep** (Chapter 23).

8. **Reduce your stress levels** (Chapter 12). If possible, agree with a friend or relative that you will take turns to massage each other on a regular basis.

9. **Make your living space clean, comfortable, and attractive.** Whenever I clean my windows or just water my plants I seem to feel much better. Display items that remind you of your achievements and the special times and people in your life.

10. **Do more of the things that you enjoy.** Go ahead and spoil yourself. Do at least one thing that you enjoy every day.

11. **Channel your inner artist**. Activities such as painting, music, poetry, and dance enable you to express yourself, interact positively with others, and reduce your stress levels. You might even impress yourself. Find a class through your local adult education service or community centre.

12. **Do some of the things you've been putting off**, like filing the paperwork, repainting the kitchen, or clearing out the garden.

13. **Set yourself a realistic challenge**. Take up yoga, learn to sing or play a song, or throw a small dinner party for some friends. In the longer term, the best way to grow our self-esteem is by bravely living up to our ideals.

14. **Be nice to people, and do nice things for them**. Strike up a conversation with the postman or shopkeeper, invite a neighbour round for tea, visit a friend who is sick, or get involved with a local charity. Putting a smile on someone's face is bound to put one on yours.

15. **Get others on board**. Tell your friends and relatives what you are going through and ask for their advice and support. Perhaps they too have similar problems, in which case you might be able to form a support group. Don't be shy or reserved: most people want to help!

16. **Spend more time with those you hold near and dear**. At the same time, try to enlarge your social circle by making an effort to meet and befriend people (Chapter 32).

17. **But avoid people and places that treat you badly or make you feel bad about yourself**. This could mean being more assertive. If assertiveness is a problem for you, ask a health professional about assertiveness training.

Finally, remember the wise words of the philosopher Lao Tzu:

Health is the greatest possession.
Contentment is the greatest treasure.
Confidence is the greatest friend.

Part 4

Mental health services and the law

36

A guide to mental health services

Fifty years ago, many people with severe depression would have been admitted to a psychiatric hospital for assessment and treatment, and some may have stayed for weeks and months. Today, people with severe depression are much more likely to remain in the community surrounded by family and friends. Hospital admission is a last resort, and, owing to a shortage of beds, lasts no longer than strictly necessary.

Modern UK mental health services reflect this emphasis on community care and are organized to encourage and support it. At the time of writing, UK mental health services are undergoing a great deal of reconfiguration. In many areas, the traditional Community Mental Health Team (CMHT) is being restructured into new specialist teams. Teams in different areas may differ quite significantly, or, more often than not, just carry different names. Figure 36.1 offers no more than a notional template.

General Practice and Accident & Emergency

Most depression that presents to medical attention is managed in general practice. If a referral to secondary care is required, this is usually to the CMHT, or, in an emergency or at night, to the crisis team.

A minority of patients first present to Accident & Emergency rather than to their GP (often because they have harmed themselves), in which case they are screened by a casualty doctor and, if it seems appropriate, referred to mental health services for further assessment and treatment.

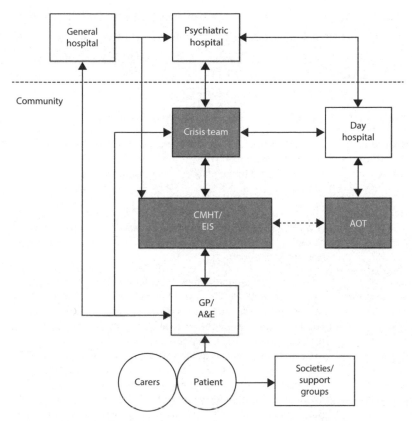

Figure 36.1:   Example of organization of mental healthcare services (local services may differ, not least in their nomenclature). Mental healthcare services are organized to avoid unnecessary hospital admissions. CMHT, Community Mental Health Team; AOT or AORT, Assertive Outreach Team; EIS, Early Intervention Service; GP, General Practice; A&E, Accident & Emergency.

Community Mental Health Team (CMHT)

The CMHT is at the centre of mental healthcare provision. It is a multidisciplinary team led by a consultant psychiatrist and operating from within the geographical sector that it serves. Community psychiatric nurses and social workers often play key roles within the CMHT, co-ordinating patient care, monitoring and supporting patients in the community, and taking referrals. Other important members of the team include more junior psychiatrists, clinical psychologists, occupational therapists, and administrative staff (Table 36.1).

Table 36.1:   Key non-medical members of the CMHT

Community psychiatric nurse	The CPN is the team member with whom the patient is likely to come into contact most often. The CPN usually visits the patient's home to facilitate the treatment plan and monitor progress.
Social worker	Sometimes a patient may be allocated a social worker instead of a CPN, in which case the social worker fulfils a role similar to that of the CPN. The social worker can also help to sort out housing and benefits.
Clinical psychologist	The clinical psychologist may spend a lot of time hearing and making sense of a patient and her carers, and also deliver talking treatments such as cognitive behavioural therapy or family therapy. People often confuse psychiatrist, psychologist, psychotherapist, and psychoanalyst. A psychiatrist is a medical doctor specialized in the diagnosis and treatment of mental disorders such as schizophrenia and depression. A clinical psychologist is an expert in human experience and behaviour. A psychotherapist is any person trained in delivering specialized talking treatments, commonly a clinical psychologist or psychiatrist. Finally, a psychoanalyst is a type of psychotherapist trained in delivering specialized talking treatments based on the psychoanalytic principles pioneered by Sigmund Freud and others.
Occupational therapist	The role of the occupational therapist is to help the patient maintain skills and develop new ones. This keeps the patient engaged and motivated, and, in the longer term, facilitates her reinsertion into the workplace.
Pharmacist	Patients with a physical illness or who are pregnant or breastfeeding may benefit from engaging with a pharmacist, who may recommend adjusting their medication.
Administrative staff	Administrative staff work at the interface between patients and team members. They are responsible for arranging appointments and are often the first port of call in an emergency.

A patient who is newly referred to the CMHT is usually assessed by a psychiatrist, sometimes in the presence of another member of the team such as a CPN or social worker. The skill mix of the multidisciplinary team means that different aspects of the patient's life can be understood, and addressed, from multiple angles.

Assertive Outreach Team (AOT or AORT)

Some people with severe mental disorder are reluctant to seek help, and as a result only appear at their CMHT in times of crisis. These so-called 'revolving door' patients, who often have the most intractable mental health and social problems, are best seen to by the AOT, a specialized multidisciplinary team dedicated to engaging them in treatment and supporting them in their daily activities.

Early Intervention Service (EIS)

Like the AOT, the EIS may also operate from the CMHT base. Its role is specifically to improve short- and long-term outcomes of psychotic disorders through a three-pronged approach involving preventative measures, earlier detection of untreated cases, and intensive treatment and support in the early stages of illness.

Crisis team

The crisis team is a 24 hours a day, 7 days a week, 365 days a year multidisciplinary team that acts as a gatekeeper to a variety of mental health services, including admission to a psychiatric hospital. Patients in a crisis are referred to the crisis team from a variety of places, most commonly GPs, A&E, and CMHTs. A member of the team, most often a CPN, promptly assesses the patient with a psychiatrist to determine if hospital admission can be prevented by short-term intensive home care. If so, the crisis team arranges for a team member to visit the patient's home up to three times a day, gradually decreasing the frequency of visits as the patient stabilizes. Other than simply providing support, the crisis team can assist in implementing a care plan and monitoring progress. It can also facilitate and expedite the discharge of in-patients.

Psychiatric hospital and day hospital

A patient requires hospital admission when community care is no longer an option, usually because:

- The patient poses a danger to herself or others, or is very vulnerable.
- The patient requires specialized care or supervised treatment.
- The patient lacks a social structure.
- Carers can no longer cope and need respite.

Some patients are admitted on an informal, that is, voluntary, basis, while others have to be admitted under a Section of the Mental Health Act (Chapter 38). In either case, a priority for the medical team is to discharge the patient as soon as practically possible.

A less restrictive option may be for the patient to attend a day hospital. The day hospital only operates within office hours, and can provide patients with daily care and structure without entirely removing them from the community.

General hospital (liaison psychiatry)

'Liaison psychiatry' (or 'psychological medicine') refers to psychiatric services within a general hospital. Since the 1970s, liaison psychiatry has evolved into a recognized sub-specialism of psychiatry, devoted to the overlap between psychiatry and the rest of medicine. At its core, it involves providing expert advice and treatment to in- and out-patients referred from other specialties, including A&E medicine. Cases vary greatly, but depression secondary to a physical disorder is very common, as is self-harm.

Carers

See Chapter 41.

Societies and support groups

See *Useful addresses* at the back of the book.

37

The Care Programme Approach (CPA)

The longer-term care and treatment of patients accepted into specialist mental health services is usually planned at one or more CPA meetings attended by the patient and her carers. These meetings are useful in establishing the context of the patient's problems; evaluating her circumstances; assessing her medical, psychological, and social needs; and formulating a detailed care plan to ensure that these needs can be met.

Other than ensuring that the patient takes her medication and is regularly reviewed by a member of the multidisciplinary team, the care plan is likely to include a number of psychosocial interventions such as a talking treatment, attendance at self-help groups, and carer education and support.

A care co-ordinator, most often a CPN or social worker, is appointed to ensure that the care plan is implemented and revised in light of changing circumstances.

At the outcome of the CPA meeting, the patient should feel that her needs and concerns have been considered, and that the care plan that she has helped to formulate reflects these in as far as possible.

38

The Mental Health Act

Some people with severe mental disorders pose a serious risk to themselves or others, but lack capacity and insight and refuse the care and treatment that they require. In most countries, there are special legal provisions to protect such people from the consequences of their mental disorder.

In England and Wales, the Mental Health Act 1983 (amended in 2007) is the principal Act governing not only the compulsory admission and detention of people to a psychiatric hospital, but also their treatment, discharge from hospital, and aftercare. People with a mental disorder as defined by the Act can be detained under the Act in the interests of their health or their safety or the safety of others. To minimize the potential for abuse, the Act specifically excludes as mental disorder dependence on alcohol or drugs.

Scotland, in contrast, is governed by the Mental Health (Care and Treatment) (Scotland) Act 2003 and Northern Ireland by the Mental Health (Northern Ireland) Order 1986. In the USA, each state produces its own mental health legislation.

It is very important to emphasize that the vast majority of people suffering with depression, even severe depression, are not detainable under the Mental Health Act, which is only considered, let alone used, in the last resort.

Two of the most common Sections of the Mental Health Act used to admit people with a mental disorder to a psychiatric hospital are the so-called Section 2 and Section 3.

Section 2

Section 2 allows for an admission for assessment and treatment that can last for up to 28 days. An application for a Section 2 is usually made by an Approved Mental Health Professional (AMHP) with special training in mental health and recommended by two doctors, at least one (and usually both) of whom must have special experience in the diagnosis and treatment of mental disorders.

Under Section 2, treatment can be given, but only in so far as it aims at treating the mental disorder or conditions directly resulting from the mental disorder (so, for example, treatment for appendicitis cannot be given under the Act).

A Section 2 can be 'discharged' or revoked at any time by the Responsible Clinician (usually the consultant psychiatrist), the hospital managers, or the nearest relative. In addition, the patient can appeal against the Section, in which case her appeal is heard by a specially constituted tribunal. The patient is represented by a solicitor who helps her to construct a case for discharge. The tribunal is by nature adversarial, and it falls upon members of the patient's care team to argue for continued detention. This can be quite trying for both claimant and care team, and can at times undermine the therapeutic relationship.

Section 2 in England and Wales is broadly equivalent to Section 26 in Scotland, except that Section 26 cannot be used to admit a patient to hospital. Instead, Section 26 tags onto Section 24 (Emergency admission to hospital) or Section 25 (Detention of patients already in hospital).

Section 3

A patient can be detained under Section 3 after a conclusive period of assessment under Section 2, or if her diagnosis has already been established by the care team and is not in reasonable doubt. Section 3 corresponds to an admission for treatment and lasts for up to six months. As for Section 2, it is usually applied for by an AMHP and approved by two doctors.

Treatment can be given only in so far as it aims at treating the mental disorder or conditions directly resulting from the mental disorder. After the first three months, any treatment requires either the consent of the patient or the recommendation of a second doctor.

A Section 3 can be discharged at any time by the Responsible Clinician, the hospital managers, or the nearest relative. In addition, the patient can appeal against the Section, in which case her appeal is heard by a specially constituted tribunal, as above.

If the patient requires detention after six months, Section 3 can be renewed for further periods.

Section 3 is broadly similar to Section 18 of the Health (Care and Treatment) (Scotland) Act 2003.

'Aftercare'

A patient under Section 3 is automatically placed under Section 117 at the time of her discharge from the Section 3. Section 117 corresponds to 'aftercare', and places a duty on services to provide the patient with a care package aimed at rehabilitation and relapse prevention. Although the patient is under no obligation to accept aftercare, in some cases she may also be placed under 'Supervised Community Treatment' or 'Guardianship' to ensure that she receives it. Under Supervised Community Treatment, she is made subject to certain conditions, which, if unmet, can result in a recall to hospital.

Police Sections: Sections 135 and 136

Section 135 of the Mental Health Act allows the removal of a person from her premises to a 'place of safety' (often a specially designated part of a psychiatric hospital), and lasts for up to 72 hours.

Section 136 allows for the removal of a person from a public place to a 'place of safety', and also lasts for up to 72 hours.

In both cases, the person must appear to the police to be suffering from a mental disorder.

Sections 135 and 136 automatically trigger an assessment under the Mental Health Act, potentially leading to a Section 2 or Section 3.

39

Driving and depression

The guidance that follows applies to the more severe forms of depression and anxiety, as well as to mania, schizophrenia, and other schizophrenia-like psychotic disorders.

You should stop driving during a first episode or relapse of your illness, because driving while ill can imperil lives. In the UK, you must notify the Driver and Vehicle Licensing Authority (DVLA). Failure to do so makes it illegal for you to drive and invalidates your insurance. Once notified, the DVLA will send you a medical questionnaire to fill out, together with a form asking for your permission to contact your psychiatrist. Your driving license can normally be reinstated if your psychiatrist can confirm that:

- Your illness has been successfully treated with medication for a certain period of time, typically three months.
- You are conscientious about taking your medication.
- Any adverse effects of your medication are unlikely to impair your driving.
- You are not misusing drugs.

People who misuse drugs should also stop driving, as should some people who suffer from other mental disorders such as dementia, learning disability, and personality disorder.

If you are in any doubt as to whether this advice applies to you—for example, if you are unsure whether your depression is severe enough to disqualify you from driving— speak to your doctor at the soonest opportunity.

Further information can be found on the DVLA website at www.dvla.gov.uk. Note that the rules for professional driving are stricter than those outlined above.

40

Social benefits

Every year in the UK, millions of pounds of social benefits are left unclaimed, often by people with chronic depression and their carers. Some of the state benefits available to you are detailed in this chapter. For further information, see the Department for Work and Pensions website, contact your local Citizens Advice Bureau, or get in touch with your local Social Services.

www.dwp.gov.uk/lifeevent/benefits

Housing Benefit and Council Tax Reduction

Housing Benefit and Council Tax Reduction are means-tested, tax-free payments made to people who need help paying their rent and council tax. From 1st January 2012, if you are single and under 35, you can only get housing benefit for bed-sit accommodation or one room in shared accommodation. Both Housing Benefit and Council Tax Reduction are administered by the local authority of the area in which your property, bedsit, or room is located. Note that these benefits cannot cover mortgage interest payments.

Employment and Support Allowance (ESA)

ESA is designed to support people under state pension age with an illness or disability that restricts their ability to work. It has replaced Incapacity Benefit, Income Support paid because of an illness or disability, and Severe Disability Allowance. ESA comprises financial help and, if appropriate, support to get back into some form of employment.

Working Tax Credit

People with an illness or disability that restricts the amount that they can earn can claim working tax credit if they are beyond the age of 16 and work an average of 16 hours a week or more.

Personal Independence Payment (PIP)

PIP is a benefit for people between the ages of 16 to 64 who because of long-term illness or disability may need help with daily activities or getting around. Unlike Disability Living Allowance, which it replaced, PIP is based on the impact rather than the nature of the disability. It is not means-tested, non-contributory, and tax-free. It is not linked to a person's ability to work, and can also be claimed by people in work.

Attendance Allowance

Attendance Allowance is paid to people aged 65 or over who need help with personal care because of an illness or disability. It is not means-tested, non-contributory, and tax-free.

Carer's Allowance

Carer's Allowance is a means-tested, taxable weekly benefit payment for people who care for someone in receipt of PIP, Attendance Allowance, or some other benefits. Among other stipulations, the carer must be over 16 years old and spend 35 hours a week or more in her caring role. She does not have to be related to, or living with, the person for whom she is caring.

Social Fund

Social Fund payments are payments, grants, or loans made in addition to certain benefits for intermittent expenses that cannot be met by normal income.

NHS costs

Depending on your circumstances, you may qualify for free NHS prescriptions and hospital medicines, free NHS dental treatment, and free NHS eyesight tests. Other NHS costs may also be met.

Universal Credit

Universal Credit is a means-tested benefit that will come to replace Housing Benefit, Child Tax Credit, income-related Employment and Support Allowance, income-based Jobseeker's Allowance, Income Support, and Working Tax Credit. Other benefits such as PIP will remain largely unchanged. Universal Credit is gradually being phased in, and the current benefits will remain for some years.

41

Advice for carers

According to Carers UK, each year in the UK over two million people take up the role of a carer. An attentive carer can be an invaluable source of structure and support for a person with depression, and her greatest hope for a long-lasting recovery. Although you may feel that caring for a loved one is more a duty than a job, it is important that you identify yourself as a carer to obtain the help and support that you are entitled to.

General principles

Learn as much as you can about depression to understand how it is affecting your loved one. For instance, she may lack spontaneity when replying to you, not because she is ignoring you, but because she is lacking in energy and concentration. Knowledge builds up your confidence as a carer and gives you a clearer sense of what you may and may not be able to expect and achieve. Remember that there is only so much that you can do to help your loved one: being realistic helps to manage stress and avoid burnout.

Caring for a person with depression is likely to require a lot of patience: progress usually comes in small steps, with both good days and bad days. A relapse is likely to sap your morale, and it's important that you prepare for this eventuality. Draw up an action plan before problems arise, and discuss it with the care team. If problems do arise, get in touch with the care team sooner rather than later. Your caring role has made you a repository of knowledge and expertise: learn to trust in your instincts and judgements.

People with depression, particularly psychotic depression, may not recognize that they are ill. If your loved one is reluctant to engage with services, try to break things down into small, manageable steps, starting with an initial doctor's appointment. If possible, give your loved one a degree of choice in booking the appointment, and offer to accompany her.

Because progress is gradual, it's easy to lose sight of the fact that progress is actually being made. Try to feel positive about your loved one, and to quietly encourage and facilitate her recovery. One of the most important things you can do is to establish a simple daily routine with regular times for eating and sleeping. Also very important is to ensure that your loved one attends her appointments and engages with her care team.

At the same time, avoid nagging, arguing, criticising, and scolding. Stress is an important predictor of relapse, and you need to make sure that your loved one has enough time and space in which to get better. At every moment, you need to create the right balance between structure and freedom, and rest and activity. Don't give in to your carer's instinct to pack in as much as possible, and be realistic about the progress that can be made. If, despite your best efforts, you are not getting on with your loved one, discuss this with a member of the care team, who may be able to offer advice, counselling, or even family therapy.

Finally, be vigilant to the needs of other family members. Children, particularly when young, may feel that they are not getting their fair share of your attention, and may grow envious and resentful (see below).

Practical support

As a carer, you can arrange an assessment of your needs by asking your GP to refer you to local Social Services or by referring yourself directly. The aim of a carer's needs assessment is to ensure that your practical needs are being met. You can find out about carer support services in your area through Social Services, a local carers' organization, or Carers UK and their phone line, CarersLine. Such services may include, among others, the provision of aids and equipment, help at home, day care, and break services. Many carers are reluctant to claim social benefits, perhaps because they have never done so, or are put off by the complicated rules and difficult forms. As a carer, you play an important role in society, and the benefits that you are entitled to exist to recognize and support that role. Most of these benefits are detailed in Chapter 40. The mental health team, Social Services, or voluntary organizations such as Carers UK can help you to claim them.

Emotional support

Remember that you are not alone as a carer. Share your thoughts and experiences with your loved one's care team and don't hesitate to ask for help and advice. Your perspective is important to the care team, so try to accompany your loved one to appointments and to take part in discussions about her care. Identify someone, perhaps a relative or friend, to talk to on a more personal level about your life as a carer. Friends and family may be reluctant to discuss your caring role, and, as a result, may underestimate your efforts and sacrifices. The onus is on you to broach the subject and enlist their support. Joining a local carers' support group enables you to meet other carers and learn from their experiences, and to find a space for negative and often unspoken emotions such as guilt, shame, anger, and exasperation.

Your physical and mental health

Carers need to look after themselves if they are to look after others. Many carers come under severe stress, eventually leading to serious health problems such as heart disease or mental disorder, including depression. It is important that you recognize this and take it seriously if you are not to become ill and unable to carry out your carer role. Use the techniques for stress management in Chapter 12 to reduce your stress levels and book an annual health check with your GP. Be good to yourself: eat healthily, exercise, pursue your hobbies, and take the occasional break or holiday from caring.

Avoiding blame

Parents sometimes think that their child's depression comes from bad parenting and feel that they are to blame. Their misplaced guilt can weigh on family life, adding to the child's already heavy burden. In some cases, parents may look around for someone to blame, such as the GP, psychiatrist, or even their own child. This is natural and understandable, and helps them to make sense of the illness. But in most cases there is, of course, no real culprit. Instead of playing the blame game and dissipating their energies, parents should focus their minds on the road to recovery.

Just like guilt and blame, anger and frustration can be normal reactions to the illness of a loved one. Parents may have thoughts such as, 'Why did this have to happen to us?' or even 'Why should I bother?' They may take out their anger and frustration on their child, even when they know that she is not to blame. Unchecked anger only adds to everyone's stress and holds your family back. Try diffusing negative feelings by talking through them with relatives, friends, the care team, and other carers. Or try channelling your anger and frustration so that they become a force for good, for example, by motivating you to seek help for your family.

Life beyond caring

As your loved one makes progress, she will become more and more independent. When this happens, you might find yourself lacking in purpose and direction, and unable to adjust to the loss of your role as a carer. Caring can be so demanding that it swallows you up. Don't allow yourself to get eaten. Throughout your time as a carer, it is vital that you keep up the other parts of your life. Many carers are able to work part-time, which is both a salutary distraction from the stress of caring and an invaluable source of income. Similarly, some carers are able to further their interests and skills, for example, by enrolling on an evening course or part-time degree.

Siblings

As parents focus their resources on their sick child, they run the risk of becoming less available to their other children. They too are in need of parental attention, and are likely to have been profoundly affected by the illness of their sibling. They may be anxious for their family and fearful of falling ill in turn. Depression often first appears at a time when young people are launching into life, starting college or university, holding down a first job, or enjoying an expanding range of activities and relationships. Brothers and sisters may find it hard to enjoy their successes while their sibling slips behind. At the same time, they may feel pressured to do more or better to 'compensate' for their sibling's illness and remove from the concerns of their afflicted parents.

Brothers and sisters should not blame themselves or anybody else for their sibling's illness or let it prevent them from enjoying their life. By nurturing outside friendships, they may be able to talk through difficult feelings and find extra emotional support. They should educate themselves about their sibling's illness and, as far as possible, involve themselves in family discussions about the road to recovery. Older siblings may like to play a more active caring role and provide their parents with support and respite. If siblings feel that they are not getting the parental attention that they need, they should not feel afraid or guilty to raise the matter with one or both parents.

Useful addresses

The Samaritans

www.samaritans.org

The Samaritans provide emotional support to anyone in emotional distress, struggling to cope, or at risk of suicide, often through their round-the-clock helpline on 116 123. 'It doesn't matter who you are, how you feel, or what has happened. If you feel that things are getting to you, get in touch.'

Papyrus

www.papyrus-uk.org

Papyrus is the national charity for the prevention of young suicide. It offers support and resources for people dealing with suicide, depression, or emotional distress, notably through HOPElineUK on 0800 068 41 41.

Cruse Bereavement Care

www.cruse.org.uk

Cruse Bereavement Care helps bereaved people to understand their grief and cope with their loss. It offers face-to-face, telephone, email, and website support through a network of 5,000 trained volunteers.

Relate

www.relate.org.uk

Relate helps people make the most of their couple and family relationships, 'past, present, and future.' Services include online information, relationship counselling for individuals and couples; family counselling; children and young people's counselling; phone, email, and Live Chat counselling; mediation, workshops; and sex therapy.

MIND (National Association for Mental Health)

www.mind.org.uk

Mind provides advice and support to anyone experiencing a mental health problem, and campaigns to improve services, raise awareness, and promote understanding. Over 180 local MIND associations run services such as floating support schemes, drop-in centres, and self-help support groups. Through its *info*Line on 0300 123 3393, MIND offers confidential help on a range of mental health issues.

Rethink Mental Illness

www.rethink.org

Rethink offers over 200 services and more than 150 support groups across England. The range of services includes advocacy, carer support, community support, and psychological therapies. Rethink runs an advice and information service on 0300 5000 927, and produces a regular magazine, *Your Voice*.

SANE

www.sane.org.uk

The work of SANE includes: campaigning for better services and treatments; initiating scientific research; and, through SANELINE and Textcare, providing information, crisis care, and emotional support to sufferers and their families and carers. The online Support Forum is a moderated peer-to-peer community. You can reach SANELINE on 0300 304 7000.

Making Space

www.makingspace.co.uk

Making Space exists to help all those suffering from mental illness. Services include carer support and respite, computerized CBT, befriending schemes, self-help groups, and volunteer projects.

Bipolar UK

www.bipolaruk.org

Bipolar UK supports people with bipolar disorder and their families and carers. Services include phone and email information and advice, support groups, an online eCommunity, one-to-one telephone mentoring, and employment support.

Anxiety UK

www.anxietyuk.org.uk

Anxiety UK provides extensive online information on anxiety disorders. Member benefits include access to the members' online community, specialist email and helpline support, and reduced cost therapy and acupuncture.

No Panic

www.nopanic.org.uk

No Panic helps people with panic attacks, phobias, and other anxiety disorders, including those who are trying to give up tranquillizers. It specializes in self-help recovery, and also offers carer support, among others. The helpline is on 0844 967 4848.

OCD Action

www.ocdaction.org.uk

OCD Action provides support and information to sufferers of OCD and related disorders. It offers, among others, local support groups, email support, and a telephone helpline on 0845 390 6232.

beat

www.b-eat.co.uk

This charity has a simple vision: eating disorder will be overcome. Services include online information and support, local support groups, and helplines for adults (0345 634 1414) and young people (0345 634 7650).

Drinkline

0300 123 1110 (9am-8pm Mon-Fri, 11am-4pm Sat-Sun)
Drinkline, the National Alcohol Helpline, offers information
and advice for people who are concerned about their drinking,
or someone else's.

Alcoholics Anonymous

www.alcoholics-anonymous.org.uk

Alcoholics Anonymous is a spiritually oriented community of
alcoholics whose aim is to stay sober and, through shared
experience and understanding, to help other alcoholics to do the
same, 'one day at a time', by avoiding that first drink. The
programme essentially involves a 'spiritual awakening' that is
achieved by 'working the steps', usually with the guidance of a
more experienced member or 'sponsor'. Members attend initially
daily meetings in which they share their experiences of
alcoholism and recovery and engage in prayer and meditation.
Alcoholics Anonymous also operate a helpline on 0800 9177 650.

Al Anon

www.al-anonuk.org.uk

Al-Anon offers understanding and support for families and
friends of problem drinkers. At Al-Anon group meetings,
members receive comfort and understanding and learn to cope
with their problems through the exchange of experience,
strength, and hope. Members learn that there are things that
they can do to help themselves and, indirectly, the problem
drinker.

Cocaine Anonymous

www.cauk.org.uk

Cocaine Anonymous is a fellowship of men and women who
share their experience, strength, and hope with one another to
solve their common problem and recover from their addiction.

The only requirement for membership is a desire to stop using cocaine and all other mind-altering substances.

Narcotics Anonymous

www.ukna.org

Narcotics Anonymous is a non-profit fellowship of men and women for whom drugs have become a major problem. Members are recovering addicts who meet regularly to help each other stay clean. The only requirement for membership is a desire to stop using drugs.

Smokefree

www.nhs.uk/smokefree

Smokefree supports people who want to stop smoking. They can choose from an app, Quit Kit, email, SMS, and face-to-face guidance.

The Sleep Council

www.sleepcouncil.com

The Sleep Council provides information and advice on improving sleep quality.

CRISIS

www.crisis.org.uk

CRISIS offers help and support to homeless people and people in danger of becoming homeless so that they can rebuild their lives and escape the cycle of homelessness.

Carers UK

www.carersuk.org

In giving so much to society, carers can fall victim to stress, ill health, poverty, and prejudice. Carers UK helps to fight these injustices by, among others, lending a voice to carers, connecting carers with one another, and providing information and support through the Carers UK adviceline, on 0808 808 7777.

By the same author

The Meaning of Madness

ISBN 978-0-9929127-3-4

This book aims to open up the debate on mental disorders, to get people interested and talking, and to get them thinking. For example, what is schizophrenia? Why is it so common? Why does it affect human beings but not other animals? What might this tell us about our mind and body, language and creativity, music and religion? What are the boundaries between mental disorder and 'normality'? Is there a relationship between mental disorder and genius? These are some of the difficult but important questions that this book confronts, with the overarching aim of exploring what mental disorders can teach us about human nature and the human condition.

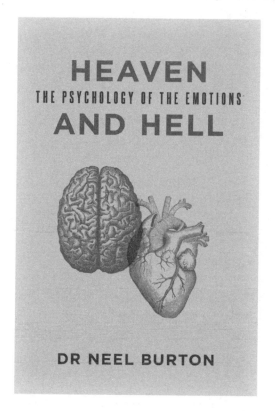

Heaven and Hell: The Psychology of the Emotions
ISBN 978-0-9929127-2-7
Many people lumber through life without giving full
consideration to their emotions, partly because our empirical,
materialistic culture does not encourage it or even make it seem
possible, and partly because it requires unusual strength to gaze
into the abyss of our deepest drives, needs, and fears. This book
proposes to do just that, examining over 25 emotions ranging
from lust to love and humility to humiliation, and drawing
some powerful and astonishing conclusions along the way.

Hide and Seek: The Psychology of Self-Deception
ISBN 978-0-9560353-6-3

Self-deception is common and universal, and the cause of most human tragedies. Of course, the science of self-deception can help us to live better and get more out of life. But it can also cast a murky light on human nature and the human condition, for example, on such exclusively human phenomena as anger, depression, fear, pity, pride, dream making, love making, and god making, not to forget age-old philosophical problems such as selfhood, virtue, happiness, and the good life. Nothing could possibly be more important.

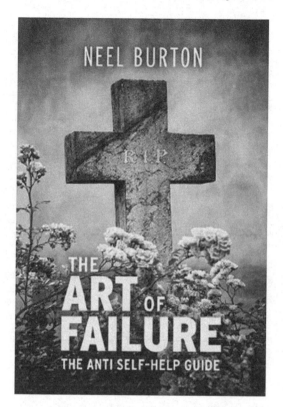

The Art of Failure: The Anti Self Help Guide
ISBN 978-0-9560353-3-2
We spend most of our time and energy chasing success, such
that we have little left over for thinking and feeling, being and
relating. As a result, we fail in the deepest possible way. We fail
as human beings.

The Art of Failure explores what it means to be successful, and
how, if at all, true success can be achieved.